by the Society of
Wine Educators

SOCIETY *of* WINE EDUCATORS

CERTIFIED
SPECIALIST
OF WINE

Jane A. Nickles

WORKBOOK
To Accompany the
2024 CSW Study Guide

INTRODUCTION TO THE CERTIFIED SPECIALIST OF WINE WORKBOOK

The Certified Specialist of Wine (CSW) credential represents the Society of Wine Educators' recognition that the holder has attained a broad base of knowledge about wine, equivalent to a midlevel wine professional. The CSW Study Guide, published by the Society of Wine Educators, is the approved study tool for the CSW and covers the depth of information needed to successfully pass the CSW Certification Exam.

This workbook is intended to accompany the 2024 version of the CSW Study Guide. Used properly, this workbook should be an invaluable tool for all CSW candidates.

The chapters in this workbook follow the chapters in the CSW Study Guide. We recommend that you first read and study a chapter in the Study Guide, and then complete the exercises in the workbook. These exercises are intended to both assess your comprehension and to increase your memory retention of the subject matter. The exercises are organized according to the major topic headings within the Study Guide itself.

After you read each chapter, try to answer the questions without consulting the Study Guide, and then check your answers by using the online answer key. Each chapter's exercises include a short "checkpoint" quiz intended to test your knowledge after you have completed your study of the chapter.

Keep in mind that while the exercises in this workbook cover much of the information found in our Study Guide, any information found in the Study Guide is considered fair game to be used as the basis for questions found on our Certified Specialist of Wine Exam.

ANSWER KEY

The answer key for this workbook is available online at SWE's blog site at http://winewitandwisdomswe.com/study-guide-updates/csw-updates/csw-workbook-answer-key/.

A NOTE ON MAPS

The maps included in the CSW Study Guide are available electronically on the membership portal of the SWE website. The maps are considered an integral part of the material in the Study Guide and form the basis for many of the exercises contained within this workbook.

This publication is intended to provide accurate information in regard to the subject matter covered; however, facts and figures regarding numbers of appellations, relative rankings of countries, and wine laws are all liable to change over time. Please contact the Society of Wine Educators if you have any questions or comments about the contents of this workbook or the accompanying CSW Study Guide.

The answer key for this workbook is available online at SWE's blog site at http://winewitandwisdomswe.com/study-guide-updates/csw-updates/csw-workbook-answer-key/

Printed in the United States of America

RESOURCES FOR CSW CANDIDATES

The Society of Wine Educators offers many resources for CSW students and exam candidates, including the following:

The Insider's Guide to the CSW Exam: Offered at least once a month, this webinar will cover all aspects of the CSW, including what the test entails, how difficult the test is, what types of questions to expect, the resources available to students, and how long SWE recommends for study before sitting for the exam. You may find the latest schedule for the Insider's Guide to the CSW Exam on the homepage of the SWE website.

Online Prep Classes: Several times a year, SWE offers guided online prep classes covering the CSW Study Guide. These classes are offered free of charge for professional members of SWE who hold a current CSW Exam attendance credit. For more information, contact Jane Nickles at jnickles@societyofwineeducators.org.

Wine and Spirits Industry Updates: To assist all members of the adult beverage industry so that they may keep up with the ever-changing world of wine and spirits, SWE maintains a list of "Wine and Spirit World Updates." Significant changes that occur in the regulatory landscape or elsewhere in the world of wine and spirits will be noted on these pages. The Wine and Spirits Industry Updates are available electronically on the member portal of the SWE website.

eBook: Our CSW Study Guide is available as an eBook on both Amazon and iTunes.

CSW Exams: The CSW Exam consists of 100 multiple-choice questions, with all question content drawn exclusively from the CSW Study Guide. Candidates are provided with one (1) hour in which to complete the exam. CSW Exams are available most days of the year throughout the world—by appointment—at Pearson VUE Testing Centers or via online proctoring. To find a Pearson VUE Center near you, use the search function on SWE's landing page at the Pearson VUE website: http://www.pearsonvue.com/societyofwineeducators/.

Exams based on the 2024 version of the CSW Study Guide will remain available through December 30, 2026.

A FINAL NOTE

We hope that this workbook is useful to you in your studies, and we wish you the best of luck as you prepare to sit for the Certification Exam. Hopefully, we will soon be able to welcome you into the ranks of Certified Specialists of Wine!

CERTIFIED
SPECIALIST
OF WINE

TABLE OF CONTENTS

SOCIETY *of* WINE EDUCATORS

LEARNING OBJECTIVES

After studying this chapter, the candidate should be able to:

- Recognize the main categories of chemical compounds in wine.
- Identify the approximate concentrations of the major components of wine.

- Describe the specific types of alcohols, acids, and sugars that are most prominent in wine.
- Discuss the types of phenolic compounds that are important in wine.

EXERCISE 1: WINE COMPONENTS: MATCHING

Match each of the following terms with its appropriate definition. Each term will be used only once.

| Water | Glycerol | Tartaric acid | Citric acid | Acetic acid |
| Ethyl alcohol | Legs | Malic acid | Lactic acid | Succinic acid |

1. _____ The most prevalent of the acids found in grapes and wine

2. _____ The component that makes up 80–90% of the volume of most wines

3. _____ Slow-moving "tears" that may appear in a wine glass after the wine is swirled

4. _____ Has little or no sensory impact on the majority of quality wines

5. _____ The component that makes up 10–15% of the volume of most wines

6. _____ A type of secondary alcohol

7. _____ A sharp-tasting acid often associated with green apples

8. _____ An acid produced via the conversion of malic acid

9. _____ An acid with a slightly bitter, slightly salty flavor

10. _____ The acid found in most types of vinegar

Please fill in the blanks or give a short answer for the following statements or questions.

1. Of the six main acids found in wine, list those that are typically found in unfermented grapes.

   _____

2. Of the acids typically found in grapes, which are found in very small quantities?

   _____

3. Which acid is known to cause deposits known as wine diamonds?

   _____

4. What is the name of the winemaking process that, in addition to changing a wine's acid components, often provides wines with a creamy texture and a buttery aroma?

   _____

5. What measurement is used to define the volume of all the acids present in a wine?

   _____

6. What does pH measure?

   _____

7. What is a typical pH measurement of a highly acidic wine?

   _____

8. What pH measurement would you expect to find in a low-acid wine?

   _____

9. What are the two main fermentable sugars found in wine grapes?

   _____

10. What term is used to describe a wine that does not contain any detectable sugar?

   _____

Match each of the following terms with its appropriate definition. Each term will be used only once.

Anthocyanins   Sulfur   Resveratrol   Acetaldehyde
Vanillin   Aldehydes   Sediment   Carbon dioxide
Esters   Tannins   Ethyl acetate   Flavonols

1. _____ Yellow pigments found in white wine

2. _____ An aromatic compound found in oak barrels

3. _____ A compound found in wine believed to be beneficial to human health

4. _____ One of the most common esters found in wine

5. _____ The specific component that gives fino Sherries their distinctive aroma

6. _____ The compounds that give red wine its red, blue, or purple hue

7. _____ Bitter compounds found in the skins, seeds, and stems of grapes

8. _____ Molecules that result from the joining of an acid and an alcohol

9. _____ Matter sometimes formed as a result of polymerization

10. _____ A preservative widely used in winemaking

11. _____ Oxidized alcohols formed when wine is exposed to air

12. _____ Promotes the release of the wine's aromatic compounds

Mark each of the following statements as true or false.

1. _____ Red wines that are highly acidic tend to appear more blue in color, whereas low-acid red wines appear more red.

2. _____ Tannins can create a textural, drying sensation on the palate.

3. _____ Madeira is an example of a wine that is produced in such a way that oxidation is encouraged and expected.

4. _____ Flavonols increase in white grapes with increased exposure to sunlight.

5. _____ Raw (untoasted) oak barrels will typically contain higher levels of vanillin than lightly toasted barrels.

6. _____ The phenolic compounds of a grape are concentrated primarily in its skin and seeds.

7. _____ Wines may become oxidized after being exposed to heat.

8. _____ It is common for winemakers to encourage the oxidation of white wines such as Chenin Blanc and Riesling by maximizing air exposure during the preliminary stages of fermentation and aging.

9. _____ Ethyl acetate imparts an aroma similar to nail polish remover or glue at very low concentrations, whereas at higher concentrations it tends to smell of dried rose petals or perfume.

10. _____ Esters represent the largest group of odiferous compounds found in wine.

11. _____ In the United States, any wine containing more than 2 ppm of sulfur dioxide is required to display the "Contains Sulfites" warning on the label.

12. _____ Normal fermentation does not produce enough carbon dioxide to make a difference in the flavor profile of a typical table wine.

1. Which of the following is the most prevalent type of acid found in both vinifera grapes and wine?
   a. Acetic acid
   b. Citric acid
   c. Tartaric acid
   d. Malic acid

2. Which of the following phenolic compounds is responsible for the bitter taste and drying textural sensation found in many red wines?
   a. Vanillin
   b. Tannin
   c. Anthocyanins
   d. Sulfites

3. Which of the following is a type of molecule that results from the joining of an acid and an alcohol?
   a. Aldehydes
   b. Sulfites
   c. Flavonols
   d. Esters

4. What is the typical pH range found in table wines?
   a. 2.5 to 3.5
   b. 1.9 to 2.7
   c. 2.9 to 3.9
   d. 3.9 to 4.7

5. What is a wine diamond?
   a. A small particle created via the crystallization of tartaric acid
   b. Tannic sediment created via polymerization
   c. A by-product of malolactic fermentation that can create a buttery aroma
   d. A by-product of the fermentation of fructose

6. What is methyl alcohol?
   a. The primary alcohol component of wine
   b. A by-product of polymerization
   c. A secondary alcohol produced via fermentation
   d. A phenolic compound that provides a citrus-fruit flavor in many wines

7. In the United States, wine containing 10 ppm or more of this compound must have a warning label.
   a. Dissolved gasses
   b. Sulfites
   c. Esters
   d. Acetic acid

8. Which of the following compounds gives red wines their red, blue, or purple hues?
   a. Anthocyanins
   b. Tannins
   c. Aldehydes
   d. Resveratrol

9. Which of the following acids, created in small amounts during typical fermentation, is found in many types of vinegar?
   a. Succinic acid
   b. Malic acid
   c. Citric acid
   d. Acetic acid

10. The two main fermentable sugars present in wine grapes include the following:
    a. Glucose and sucrose, also known as monosaccharides
    b. Sucrose and fructose, also known as disaccharides
    c. Glucose and fructose, also known as monosaccharides
    d. Fructose and maltose, also known as sugar alcohols

WINE FAULTS

CHAPTER TWO

LEARNING OBJECTIVES

After studying this chapter, the candidate should be able to:

- Recall the main terminology associated with wine faults.

- Describe the source and effect of cork taint.
- Discuss the impact of sulfur compounds on wine.
- Recognize which odors are acceptable and under which conditions.

EXERCISE 1: WINE FAULTS: MATCHING

Match each of the following wine faults and off-odors with its most likely source. Terms may be used more than once.

Sulfur compounds
Bacteria
Yeast
Mold
Oxidation

1. _____ Acetic acid

2. _____ Pronounced odor of lees

3. _____ Acetaldehyde

4. _____ Mercaptan

5. _____ Cork taint

6. _____ Ascensence

7. _____ Butyric acid

8. _____ Browning

9. _____ Brettanomyces

10. _____ Geranium

Please fill in the blanks or give a short answer for the following statements or questions.

1. What compound is the root cause of cork taint?

   _____

2. What specific terms can be used to describe the aroma of a "corked" wine?

   _____

3. What substance can cause a wine to smell like rancid butter?

   _____

4. What wine fault can be caused by the interaction of sorbic acid and lactic acid bacteria?

   _____

5. What is the term used to describe a wine that has a cooked or baked odor?

   _____

6. What wine fault is typically caused by high amounts of both acetic acid and ethyl acetate?

   _____

7. What specific terms can be used to describe a wine with an excess of Brett?

   _____

8. What substance can cause a wine to smell like onions or garlic?

   _____

9. What aroma can be caused by an excess of ethyl acetate?

   _____

10. What wine fault can be described as having the aroma of burnt matches?

    _____

11. What wine fault is often described as similar to rotten eggs?

    _____

12. What off-odor is caused by acetic acid?

    _____

1. Which of the following wine odors can occur as a result of prolonged contact with dead yeast cells?
   a. Ethyl acetate
   b. Leesy
   c. Geranium
   d. Onions or garlic

2. Which of the following wine faults can occur as a result of sulfur compounds?
   a. Butyric acid
   b. Oxidation
   c. Lactic acid
   d. Mercaptan

3. Which of the following wine faults can occur as a result of an excess of Brettanomyces?
   a. Sweaty or horsy odor
   b. Citric or lemony aroma
   c. Rancid butter or spoiled cheese odor
   d. Vinegar odor

4. Which of the following compounds is responsible for cork taint?
   a. Acetic acid
   b. 2,4,6-Trichloroanisole
   c. Butyric acid
   d. Hydrogen sulfide

5. What aroma can be caused by an excess of ethyl acetate?
   a. Geranium
   b. Wet cardboard
   c. Vinegar
   d. Fingernail polish remover

6. Which of the following wine faults may be caused by lactic acid bacteria interacting with sorbic acid?
   a. Wet cardboard
   b. Oxidized
   c. Geranium
   d. Brett

7. TCA is noticeable at very _____ concentrations, with most people able to detect it at the level of _____
   a. Low, 2 to 7 parts per trillion
   b. Low, 100 to 120 parts per trillion
   c. High, 2,000 to 5,000 parts per million
   d. High, 10,000 to 20,000 parts per million

8. What wine fault can lead to the aroma of rotten eggs?
   a. Brettanomyces
   b. Hydrogen sulfide
   c. Ethyl acetate
   d. Mercaptan

GRAPE VARIETIES

CHAPTER THREE

LEARNING OBJECTIVES

After studying this chapter, the candidate should be able to:

- State the differences between *Vitis vinifera* and other vine species.
- Discuss hybrids, crossings, and clones.
- Describe the primary characteristics of the classic international white grape varieties.
- Describe the primary characteristics of the classic international red grape varieties.

EXERCISE 1: GRAPEVINE SPECIES AND VARIETIES: MATCHING

Match each of the following terms with its appropriate definition. Terms may be used more than once.

Cross	Variety	Autochthonous	Species	Hybrid
Mutation	Seyval Blanc	Cabernet Sauvignon	International	Clone

1. _____ An example of a hybrid grape

2. _____ An example of a grape that was produced via a crossing

3. _____ A scientific grouping of plants or animals that are genetically similar and can produce viable offspring via sexual reproduction

4. _____ The name for the category of grapes that result from the sexual reproduction between a *Vitis vinifera* grape and a *Vitis labrusca* grape

5. _____ Term used for the offspring of sexual reproduction between two *Vitis vinifera* grapes

6. _____ Term used for a subspecies of *Vitis vinifera*

7. _____ Term used for indigenous grapes that are the result of natural cross-breeding or natural mutation in a specific area

8. _____ A term used for grape varieties that have been found to thrive in a wide range of environments

9. _____ Term used for an asexually reproduced vine that has modified itself to be slightly different from its parent

10. _____ A grape variety derived from a vine that has different characteristics from its parents via imperfect reproduction of its cells as it grows

11. _____ A type of grape variety that often has a number assigned to it

12. _____ A grape that is a result of the sexual reproduction of grapes from two different but closely related species

EXERCISE 2: WHITE GRAPE VARIETIES: MATCHING

Match each of the following wine-producing areas with the grape variety from the list with which it is most closely associated.

Chardonnay	Pinot Gris	Semillon	Ugni Blanc
Chenin Blanc	Riesling	Viognier	Torrontés
Muscat	Sauvignon Blanc	Albariño	Furmint

1. _____ Argentina

2. _____ Northern Rhône

3. _____ Hunter Valley (Australia)

4. _____ Burgundy

5. _____ Rutherglen (Australia)

6. _____ Cognac

7. _____ Sancerre

8. _____ Eden Valley (Australia)

9. _____ Northeast Italy; Oregon (United States)

10. _____ Vouvray

11. _____ Spain

12. _____ Hungary

13. _____ Pouilly-Fumé

14. _____ Savennières

EXERCISE 3: RED GRAPE VARIETIES: TRUE OR FALSE

Mark each of the following statements as true or false.

1. _____ Tempranillo is the sole ingredient in many of the red wines of Piedmont, Italy.

2. _____ Zinfandel is known for producing robust red wines as well as off-dry blush wines.

3. _____ Merlot ripens late, and Cabernet Sauvignon ripens early.

4. _____ Cabernet Sauvignon, Cabernet Franc, and Merlot are all grown in Bordeaux.

5. _____ Cabernet Sauvignon is the most widely planted quality red grape in the world.

6. _____ The Chinon AOC produces a red wine based on Cabernet Franc.

7. _____ Merlot is known as Spätburgunder in Germany.

8. _____ Grenache is grown in the Spanish region of Priorat.

9. _____ Zinfandel is believed to be native to the Dalmatian Coast of Croatia, where it goes by the name *Tribidag*.

10. _____ Pinot Noir is grown in the Champagne region of France.

11. _____ Malbec is referred to as Cannonau on the island of Sardinia.

12. _____ Sangiovese is the main grape variety used in the wines of the Chianti DOCG.

13. _____ Tempranillo is not grown in Portugal.

14. _____ Syrah and Shiraz are actually the same grape variety.

15. _____ Barolo is made from 100% Nebbiolo.

Name the grape varieties described by the following statements.

1. _____ Italian variety known to have aromas of tar and roses

2. _____ The main variety in "the black wine of Cahors"

3. _____ White grape variety that can be coaxed into a wide variety of styles, including a "California style" that often has aromas of butterscotch, vanilla, and tropical fruit

4. _____ Also known as Pinot Grigio

5. _____ Red grape grown in Burgundy, New Zealand, and Oregon

6. _____ Italian variety known to have a characteristic sour cherry and orange peel flavor profile

7. _____ The leading red grape of Spain

8. _____ Also known as Ugni Blanc

9. _____ One of the most aromatic white grape varieties, known for aromas of perfume, flowers, spice, lychee, and rose

10. _____ Red grape variety often used in a blend along with Grenache and Mourvèdre

11. _____ Widely planted white grape variety known for aromas of musk, honey, apricot, table grapes, and orange blossom

12. _____ Red grape variety that is native to France, but that has achieved renown in Argentina

13. _____ White grape that often shows gasoline- or petrol-like aromas

14. _____ Also known as Weissburgunder

15. _____ The most widely planted grape in South Africa

1. Which of the following is true concerning Seyval Blanc and Baco Noir grapes?
   a. They are *Vitis labrusca* varieties.
   b. They are *Vitis vinifera* varieties.
   c. They are hybrids.
   d. They are clones.

2. The term *vinifera* refers to which of the following categories?
   a. A grapevine species
   b. A grapevine variety
   c. A grapevine family
   d. A grapevine genus

3. Which of the following grapes is primarily grown in Piedmont, Italy?
   a. Cabernet Sauvignon
   b. Chenin Blanc
   c. Sauvignon Blanc
   d. Nebbiolo

4. Which of the following grapes is also known as Grauburgunder?
   a. Pinot Noir
   b. Pinot Gris
   c. Chardonnay
   d. Pinot Blanc

5. Which of the following grape varieties is known for showing fruity, mineral, and petrol-like aromas?
   a. Chenin Blanc
   b. Viognier
   c. Sauvignon Blanc
   d. Riesling

6. Which of the following wines is made from a majority of Cabernet Franc?
   a. Left Bank Bordeaux
   b. Morgon
   c. Chinon
   d. Vouvray

7. Which of the following wines is most likely made from a majority of Merlot?
   a. Right Bank Bordeaux
   b. Left Bank Bordeaux
   c. Rioja
   d. Chianti

8. Which of the following is the leading red grape of Australia?
   a. Merlot
   b. Cabernet Sauvignon
   c. Syrah
   d. Zinfandel

9. Australia's Hunter Valley is best known for which of the following grape varieties?
   a. Semillon
   b. Sauvignon Blanc
   c. Torrontés
   d. Chenin Blanc

10. Chenin Blanc is the most widely grown grape variety in which of the following countries?
    a. France
    b. Spain
    c. Argentina
    d. South Africa

11. Which of the following grapes is native to France, but is now grown extensively in Argentina?
    a. Merlot
    b. Malbec
    c. Pinot Noir
    d. Zinfandel

12. Which of the following grapes is also known as Ugni Blanc?
    a. Chardonnay
    b. Chenin Blanc
    c. Trebbiano Toscano
    d. Sauvignon Blanc

13. Which of the following grapes is also sometimes referred to as Cannonau?
    a. Cabernet Sauvignon
    b. Merlot
    c. Malbec
    d. Grenache

14. Which of the following regions produces a well-known wine from the Malbec grape variety?
    a. Cahors
    b. Montalcino
    c. Priorat
    d. Morgon

VITICULTURE

CHAPTER FOUR

LEARNING OBJECTIVES

After studying this chapter, the candidate should be able to:

- Describe the physical structure of a grapevine.
- Explain the annual life cycle and metabolic processes of the vine.
- Identify the factors that affect the amount of sugar and acid in grapes.
- Recognize the elements that make up the concept of terroir.
- Recall the effects of vine diseases, pests, and botrytis.
- Understand how viticultural practices such as organic, biodynamic, and sustainable differ from those of mainstream viticulture and from each other.

EXERCISE 1: GROWTH CYCLE OF THE VINE: TIMELINE

Put the following stages of the annual growth cycle of the vine in chronological order, starting with winter dormancy and following through the year.

Berry set

Photosynthesis begins

Harvest

Bud break

Phenolic maturity

Veraison

Shoot and leaf growth

Flowering

Weeping

1. Winter dormancy _____

2. _____

3. _____

4. _____

5. _____

6. _____

7. _____

8. _____

9. _____

10. _____

EXERCISE 2: THE VINE'S METABOLIC PROCESSES: SHORT ANSWER/FILL IN THE BLANK

Name the metabolic processes described by the following statements.

1. _____ The process by which materials are moved from one part of the plant to another

2. _____ The process by which sunlight is converted into sugar

3. _____ The process by which water evaporates through openings on the underside of the leaves

4. _____ The process by which sugar is broken down and converted into biological energy

EXERCISE 3: VINE PESTS, PROBLEMS, AND DISEASES: MATCHING

Match each of the following vine maladies with its appropriate definition. Each term will be used only once.

Oidium	Peronospora	Botrytis cinerea	Millerandage
Coulure	Pierce's disease	Phylloxera	Nematode

1. _____ A problem that causes poor fruit set, also known as shatter

2. _____ A soil-based roundworm that has become more prevalent with the increased use of shallow-rooted rootstock

3. _____ A mold that is sometimes beneficial, also known as noble rot

4. _____ A fungal disease also known as powdery mildew

5. _____ A problem with abnormal fruit set that causes grape bunches to have a high proportion of small, seedless berries mixed in with normal, larger berries

6. _____ A fungal disease also known as downy mildew

7. _____ A bacterial disease spread by insects such as the glassy-winged sharpshooter

8. _____ A destructive louse that feeds off the roots of vinifera vines

Please fill in the blanks or give a short answer for the following statements or questions.

1. What is the difference between climate and weather?

   _____

   _____

   _____

2. How much water do grapevines need on an annual basis?

   _____

3. Explain why soils with low fertility are generally ideal for commercial vineyards.

   _____

   _____

   _____

4. Put these four soil types in order, from smallest in particle size to largest: gravel, silt, clay, and sand.

   _____

   _____

5. Describe the potential climatic differences between a vineyard situated at a high elevation and one situated on a valley floor.

   _____

   _____

   _____

6. Explain the effect that large bodies of water have on the climate of a nearby vineyard.

   _____

   _____

   _____

EXERCISE 5: VITICULTURE: TRUE OR FALSE

Mark each of the following statements as true or false.

1. _____   In general, a lower latitude translates into a warmer climate.

2. _____   The Oechsle system of measuring grape ripeness is widely used in France.

3. _____   Photosynthesis slows, but does not stop, at night.

4. _____   The annual growth cycle of the vine is considered to begin each year with bud break, which starts once temperatures reach 65°F (18°C) in the spring.

5. _____   When producing dry table wines, the typical time from bud break to harvest is 140 to 160 days.

6. _____   Ideally, soil should enable the vine's roots to access water when needed, but also ensure that excess water is drained away.

7. _____   In the Northern Hemisphere, a vineyard on a slope that faces north gets the most sun.

8. _____   Regions with a continental climate generally experience hotter summers and colder winters than regions with a Mediterranean climate.

9. _____   Transpiration is the process by which water evaporates through openings on the underside of the leaves known as stomata.

10. _____   A Mediterranean climate is considered to have too short a growing season in order for grapes to ripen on a regular basis.

11. _____   In general, sugar as measured by degrees Brix will convert to alcohol by a conversion factor of 55%.

12. _____   Photosynthesis tends to slow down at temperatures below 50°F/10°C.

13. _____   A refractometer is used to measure the amount of rainfall that penetrates the topsoil to a depth of 6 inches (15 centimeters).

14. _____   Head-trained vines—sometimes referred to as gobelet-style vines—do not typically require vine trellis systems.

1. Which of the following statements is true concerning photosynthesis?
   a. Photosynthesis occurs most efficiently when the daytime temperature is over 90°F (32°C).
   b. Photosynthesis occurs most efficiently when the daytime temperature is under 50°F (10°C).
   c. Photosynthesis slows but does not completely shut down at night.
   d. Photosynthesis can only occur when the sun is shining.

2. In general, how much water do vines need on an annual basis?
   a. 5 to 10 inches (13–25 cm)
   b. 10 to 20 inches (25–51 cm)
   c. 20 to 30 inches (51–76 cm)
   d. 50 to 60 inches (127–152 cm)

3. Which of the following best describes the vine process of veraison?
   a. Tiny shoots start to emerge from nodes in the vine's branches, soon growing to full canopy.
   b. The grapes begin a sudden acceleration toward maturation and begin to take on color.
   c. Carbohydrate reserves stored the previous year are directed toward rapid leaf and shoot growth.
   d. The acid level of the grapes starts to rapidly increase, while sugar levels drop.

4. Which of the following are considered the ideal latitudes for commercial wine grape growing in both the Northern and Southern Hemispheres?
   a. Between 10 and 30 degrees
   b. Between 20 and 40 degrees
   c. Between 25 and 45 degrees
   d. Between 30 and 50 degrees

5. Which of the following vineyard diseases is easily spread by the glassy-winged sharpshooter?
   a. Phylloxera
   b. Powdery mildew
   c. Pierce's disease
   d. Oidium

6. Which of the following represents the correct progression of the life cycle of a grapevine?
   a. Bud break, shoot and leaf growth, flowering, berry set, veraison, harvest
   b. Bud break, berry set, flowering, shoot and leaf growth, harvest, veraison
   c. Bud break, shoot and leaf growth, flowering, berry set, harvest, veraison
   d. Bud break, flowering, shoot and leaf growth, berry set, veraison, harvest

7. Which of the following vine conditions is sometimes beneficial, and may be referred to as "noble rot"?
   a. Oidium
   b. Peronospora
   c. Botrytis
   d. Coulure

8. Which of the following is a vine metabolic process in which sugar is broken down and converted into biological energy?
   a. Respiration
   b. Transpiration
   c. Translocation
   d. Photosynthesis

9. Which of the following temperatures signals the beginning of bud break in the spring?
   a. 40°F (4.5°C)
   b. 50°F (10°C)
   c. 60°F (16°C)
   d. 70°F (21°C)

10. Which of the following soil types has the smallest particle size?
    a. Sand
    b. Clay
    c. Silt
    d. Rocks

FERMENTATION AND STILL WINE PRODUCTION

CHAPTER FIVE

LEARNING OBJECTIVES

After studying this chapter, the candidate should be able to:

- Recall the sequence of events that take place during the winemaking process.
- Recognize key terminology associated with fermentation and wine production.
- Understand the differences between red, white, and rosé winemaking.
- Describe the procedures for making sweet wines.
- Discuss what makes organic, biodynamic, and kosher wines different from other wines.

EXERCISE 1: WHITE WINE PRODUCTION: TIMELINE

Put the following stages of white wine production in typical chronological order, starting with the harvest and following through the winemaking process. Note that many of these techniques are optional and therefore not always used in the winemaking process.

Sur lie aging	Clarification	Pressing	Juice settling	Blending
Sorting	Cold stabilization	Bottling	Inoculation	
Crushing	Barrel aging	Must adjustments	Fermentation	

1. Harvest _____

2. _____

3. _____

4. _____

5. _____

6. _____

7. _____

8. _____

9. _____

10. _____

11. _____

12. _____

13. _____

14. _____

Put the following stages of red wine production in typical chronological order, starting with the harvest and following through the winemaking process. Note that many of these techniques are optional and therefore not always used in the winemaking process.

Crushing/destemming	Pressing	Inoculation	Must adjustments
Clarification	Bottling	Fermentation	Sorting
Extended maceration	Cold soak	Blending	
Barrel aging	Cap management		

1. Harvest _____

2. _____

3. _____

4. _____

5. _____

6. _____

7. _____

8. _____

9. _____

10. _____

11. _____

12. _____

13. _____

14. _____

Match each of the following terms with its appropriate definition. Each term will be used only once.

Carbonic maceration Free run   Chaptalization   Racking   Délestage
Barrique   Pomace   Bâtonnage   Fining   Pigéage
Débourbage   Must   Diacetyl   Sur lie aging

1. _____ A standard size (60 gallon/225 liter) oak barrel

2. _____ Letting the newly-pressed juice settle for a day or two before fermentation is allowed to begin

3. _____ Adding sugar to the must before fermentation begins

4. _____ Allowing the wine to rest on the dead yeast cells after fermentation has completed

5. _____ The stirring up of the dead yeast cells back into the liquid

6. _____ Grape juice, or the mixture of grape juice, seeds, and skins, that will be fermented and transformed into wine

7. _____ A chemical by-product of malolactic fermentation that imparts a buttery aroma to wine

8. _____ An enzymatic fermentation that occurs in the absence of oxygen within whole, unbroken grapes

9. _____ French term for "punching down"

10. _____ The cake of compressed grape skins and seeds that remains behind after the final pressing of the juice or wine

11. _____ The use of gravity to remove suspended matter in a batch of newly fermented wine

12. _____ A clarification technique that uses an inert material to attract and bind to unwanted materials

13. _____ French term for "rack and return"

14. _____ The first juice to run out of the press, typically considered to be of the highest quality

For each of the following wine production processes, determine whether they are likely to be used in the production of red, white, or rosé styles of wine. Place a check mark in the column of every wine type that is likely to use each process.

Process	Red?	White?	Rosé?
1. Saignée	☐	☐	☐
2. De-stemming	☐	☐	☐
3. Cap management	☐	☐	☐
4. Fermentation at 50°F (10°C)	☐	☐	☐
5. Malolactic fermentation	☐	☐	☐
6. Sulfur additions	☐	☐	☐
7. Barrel aging	☐	☐	☐
8. Fermentation at 95°F (32°C)	☐	☐	☐
9. Extended maceration	☐	☐	☐
10. Must adjustments	☐	☐	☐
11. Direct press	☐	☐	☐
12. Blending	☐	☐	☐

EXERCISE 5: WINEMAKING PRACTICES: TRUE OR FALSE

Mark each of the following statements as true or false.

1. _____ Sulfur can be added at many points during the winemaking process.

2. _____ A type of spirit called grappa is often made from the leftovers of wine production.

3. _____ Chaptalization is used to produce a wine with high levels of residual sugar.

4. _____ France and Canada are the two primary sources for oak barrels used in American wine production.

5. _____ Dessert wines are produced in the Sauternes region of France using grapes that have been affected by *Botrytis cinerea*.

6. _____ Italy's famous Amarone wine is made using grapes that have frozen naturally on the vine.

7. _____ Weissherbst is a type of German rosé.

8. _____ A mevushal wine is a kosher wine that is free from limitations on who may handle the wine once it leaves the winery.

9. _____ The direct press method of rosé production is used to create pink wines with a deep rosy hue.

10. _____ The Riesling grape variety is often used in the production of Eiswein.

11. _____ In the production of orange wines, juice from white grapes spends a period of time ranging from several days to several months macerating with the grape skins.

12. _____ Malolactic fermentation is used more often on red wines than white wines.

13. _____ Most of the yeasts used in winemaking are strains of *Saccharomyces cerevisiae*.

14. _____ Malolactic fermentation is an optional winemaking process that converts lactic acid into malic acid, resulting in a shaper, more acidic wine.

1. Which of the following types of wine are most likely to be produced using the process of saignée?
   a. Orange wines and sweet white wines
   b. Deep red wines and light rosé
   c. Crisp, dry white wines and very pale rosé
   d. Blanc de blancs sparkling wines

2. Which of the following terms is used to refer to the process of allowing newly-pressed juice to settle for a day or two before fermentation is allowed to begin?
   a. Débourbage
   b. Chaptalization
   c. Bâtonnage
   d. Stabilization

3. What is chaptalization?
   a. Adjusting the juice for acid before fermentation begins
   b. The use of oak chips or wood tannin during primary fermentation
   c. Adding sugar to the juice in order to boost alcohol content in the finished wine
   d. Allowing the grape stems to be crushed into the juice in order to increase tannin content

4. Which of the following is a chemical by-product of malolactic fermentation that often imparts a buttery aroma to wine?
   a. Succinic acid
   b. Diacetyl
   c. Aldehyde
   d. Hydrogen sulfide

5. Which of the following terms is used for the cake of compressed grape skins and seeds that remains behind after the final pressing of the juice or wine?
   a. Must
   b. Pomace
   c. Lees
   d. Free run

6. Which of the following terms is used for the mixture of juice, skins, and seeds that will be fermented into wine?
   a. Pomace
   b. Must
   c. Brett
   d. Vin gris

7. Which of the following processes uses whole, uncrushed grape clusters?
   a. Malolactic fermentation
   b. Secondary fermentation
   c. Carbonic maceration
   d. Bâtonnage

8. Very pale rosé is often produced in Provence using which of the following methods?
   a. Mutage
   b. Carbonic maceration
   c. Direct press
   d. Malolactic fermentation

9. What is sur lie aging?
   a. Using an inert material such as gelatin or egg whites to help clarify the wine
   b. Chilling the wine to around 32°F/0°C in order to prevent the formation of tartrates
   c. Using a centrifuge to clarify the wine
   d. Allowing the newly-fermented wine to rest on the dead yeast cells for a period of time

10. The mass of grape solids and skins that rises to the top of the fermentation tank during red wine fermentation is known by which of the following terms?
    a. The cap
    b. Délestage
    c. Pomace
    d. Barrique

SPARKLING WINE PRODUCTION

LEARNING OBJECTIVES

After studying this chapter, the candidate should be able to:

- Describe how sparkling wines are produced.
- Identify which grape varieties are commonly used in sparkling wines.
- Recall the sequence of events that takes place during the traditional sparkling wine production process.
- Recognize the different style categories of sparkling wines.
- Recall the terminology relating to sparkling wines.

EXERCISE 1: SPARKLING WINE PRODUCTION: MATCHING

Match each of the following terms with its appropriate definition. Each term will be used only once.

Dégorgement	Assemblage	Autolysis	Cuve close
Prise de mousse	Sur lie	Pupitre	
Remuage	Liqueur de tirage	Liqueur d'expédition	

1. _____   Added to the cuvée in order to initiate the second fermentation

2. _____   Turning the bottles and gently shaking them in order to get the dead yeast cells collected near the cap

3. _____   Time spent aging the wine on the yeast lees

4. _____   A rack used to hold bottles of wine during the riddling process

5. _____   The creation of the blended wine that will undergo a second fermentation and be turned into a sparkling wine

6. _____   The second alcoholic fermentation

7. _____   The process wherein the yeast cells begin to decompose and release their flavors

8. _____   An addition added just after disgorging a bottle of sparkling wine; also known as the dosage

9. _____   The process in which the bottle is opened and the yeast extracted

10. _____   Another name for the Charmat method of sparkling wine production

EXERCISE 2: SWEETNESS LEVELS OF SPARKLING WINE: SHORT ANSWER/FILL IN THE BLANK

Place the names of the styles of sparkling wine, listed below, in order from driest to sweetest.

Sec	Doux	Brut nature	Brut
Extra dry	Extra brut	Demi-sec	

Driest: 1. _____

2. _____

3. _____

4. _____

5. _____

6. _____

Sweetest: 7. _____

EXERCISE 3: TRADITIONAL CHAMPAGNE BOTTLE SIZES: SHORT ANSWER/FILL IN THE BLANK

Fill in the blanks with the appropriate term for the different sizes of traditional Champagne bottles.

1. _____ Equivalent to 2 standard bottles

2. _____ Equivalent to 4 standard bottles

3. _____ Equivalent to 6 standard bottles

4. _____ Equivalent to 8 standard bottles

5. _____ Equivalent to 12 standard bottles

6. _____ Equivalent to 16 standard bottles

7. _____ Equivalent to 20 standard bottles

Mark each of the following statements as true or false.

1. _____ The term *autolysis* is used to refer to the decomposition of yeast cells during the process of sur lie aging.

2. _____ The traditional Champagne press is a wide, flat basket press, and many of them are still in use today.

3. _____ The base wine that will be used in the production of Champagne is generally left very sweet.

4. _____ A blanc de blancs sparkling wine is produced using just red grape varieties.

5. _____ Most Cava is technically blanc de noirs.

6. _____ Moscato d'Asti is produced using the partial fermentation method.

7. _____ The ancestral method of sparkling wine production is sometimes referred to as the *méthode rurale*.

8. _____ The term "California Champagne" may be used on some California wine labels, but only if approved before March 10, 2012.

9. _____ Most "house style" sparkling wines are blanc de blancs, extra dry, and produced using the grapes of just one vintage.

10. _____ The second fermentation of a sparkling wine generally increases the alcohol content by one or two percentage points.

11. _____ The typical pressure of the dissolved carbon dioxide in a bottle of sparkling wine is about 10 atmospheres of pressure.

12. _____ In many bottles of sparkling wine, the cork is held in place by a wire cage known as a *muselet*.

13. _____ The tank process of sparkling wine production is used to create a wine that emphasizes youthful, floral, and primary fruit aromas.

14. _____ The most expensive method of making a sparkling wine is to inject carbon dioxide directly into a still wine.

15. _____ Chenin Blanc is often used to create sparkling wines in the Loire Valley.

1. Which of the following styles of sparkling wine has the highest level of potential residual sugar?
   a. Brut
   b. Demi-sec
   c. Extra dry
   d. Sec

2. Which of the following bottles is the largest?
   a. Magnum
   b. Rehoboam
   c. Jeroboam
   d. Nebuchadnezzar

3. Which of the following is added to a bottle of sparkling wine after the wine is disgorged?
   a. Liqueur d'expédition
   b. Cuve close
   c. Transversage
   d. Liqueur de tirage

4. Which of the following styles of sparkling wine is made using just white grape varieties?
   a. Cava
   b. Blanc de Noirs
   c. Blanc de Blancs
   d. Nonvintage

5. Which of the following styles of Champagne is most likely to be considered a brand's "house style" and most consistent wine?
   a. Vintage
   b. Blanc de Blancs
   c. Rosé
   d. Nonvintage

6. Which of the following terms is used to describe the second fermentation of a bottle of traditional method sparkling wine?
   a. Débourbage
   b. Prise de mousse
   c. Transversage
   d. Assemblage

7. What is a pupitre?
   a. A wooden rack used to hold bottles of sparkling wine during the riddling process
   b. A large machine used to mechanically rotate bottles of sparkling wine before disgorging
   c. A table used for sorting grapes prior to the crush
   d. A term used to describe the last juice pressed from grapes; destined to be used in the production of sweet sparkling wines.

8. Which of the following is the most accurate definition of a tête de cuvee wine?
   a. A sparkling wine that undergoes a second fermentation in the bottle
   b. The top-of-the-line sparkling wine produced by a given brand or producer
   c. A vintage sparkling wine made from 100% Chardonnay grapes
   d. A sparkling wine produced via assemblage

9. What is the French term for riddling?
   a. Autolysis
   b. Assemblage
   c. Remuage
   d. Cuve close

10. Which of the following represents the steps in the traditional method of sparkling wine production in the proper order?
    a. First fermentation, blending, bottling, second fermentation, riddling, disgorging, dosage
    b. First fermentation, bottling, second fermentation, blending, riddling, disgorging, dosage
    c. First fermentation, blending, second fermentation, bottling, dosage, riddling, disgorging
    d. First fermentation, bottling, second fermentation, dosage, riddling, blending, disgorging

FORTIFIED WINE PRODUCTION

LEARNING OBJECTIVES

After studying this chapter, the candidate should be able to:
- Recall the historical purpose for fortifying wines.
- Discuss how the fortified winemaking process differs from standard table wine production.
- Recognize the differences in the production methods of sweet and dry fortified wines.
- Identify the grape varieties commonly used in fortified wines.
- Describe how the solera system works.

EXERCISE 1: FORTIFIED WINE PRODUCTION: MATCHING

Fill in the blanks by matching each of the following fortified wines with its country or region of origin. Terms may be used more than once.

France   Spain   Cyprus   Greece   Italy   Portugal   Australia

1. _____ Commandaria

2. _____ Marsala

3. _____ Mavrodaphne of Patras

4. _____ Banyuls

5. _____ Rutherglen Muscat

6. _____ Muscat de Beaumes-de-Venise

7. _____ Port

8. _____ Madeira

9. _____ Málaga

10. _____ Setúbal

11. _____ Rasteau

12. _____ Maury

Fill in the blanks or give a short answer for the following statements or questions.

1. What is the term used for the process of fortified wine production in which alcohol is added to a fermenting wine while it still has a significant amount of sugar in it?

   _____

2. What grape variety is most widely used in the production of Sherry?

   _____

3. What two grape varieties are most commonly used in the production of dry styles of Madeira?

   _____

4. What style of Sherry is aged in the presence of flor yeast?

   _____

5. What style of Sherry is aged without the presence of flor yeast?

   _____

6. What type of aging occurs as a result of flor yeast?

   _____

7. What type of aging occurs when Sherry is allowed direct exposure to air?

   _____

8. What is the name of the complex network of barrels that is used to age Sherry?

   _____

9. What specific term is used for a French wine made by fortifying unfermented grape juice or must?

   _____

10. Where is Banyuls produced?

   _____

1. Which of the following is a fortified wine produced in Italy?
   a. Marsala
   b. Pineau des Charentes
   c. Setúbal
   d. Málaga

2. Sherry is aged and blended using a complex network of barrels known collectively as:
   a. Lagares
   b. The criadera system
   c. The chai
   d. The solera system

3. What style of Sherry is aged in the presence of flor yeast?
   a. Muscat Sherry
   b. Fino Sherry
   c. Cream Sherry
   d. Oloroso Sherry

4. Which of the following is a vin doux naturel produced in France?
   a. Setúbal
   b. Muscat de Beaumes-de-Venise
   c. Coteaux du Layon
   d. Sauternes

5. Which of the following fortified wines is a specialty of Cyprus?
   a. Rutherglen Muscat
   b. Rasteau
   c. Commandaria
   d. Maury

6. Which of the following is produced in the Cognac region?
   a. Muscat de Beaumes-de-Venise
   b. Commandaria
   c. Málaga
   d. Pineau des Charentes

7. The process of adding alcohol to a batch of fermenting wine while it still contains a significant amount of sugar is known by which of the following terms?
   a. Assemblage
   b. Mutage
   c. Oxidation
   d. Maceration

8. Which of the following is true concerning oloroso Sherry?
   a. It is made using a blend of red and white grapes.
   b. It is allowed to undergo oxidative aging.
   c. It is generally light in body and pale in color as compared to other styles of Sherry.
   d. It is aged in the presence of flor yeast.

9. Which of the following grape varieties is most widely used in the production of dry Madeira?
   a. Pedro Ximénez
   b. Palomino
   c. Airén
   d. Sercial

10. Which of the following grape varieties is most widely used in the production of Sherry?
   a. Palomino
   b. Tempranillo
   c. Pedro Ximénez
   d. Garnacha

INTRODUCTION TO THE WORLD WINE INDUSTRY

CHAPTER EIGHT

LEARNING OBJECTIVES

After studying this chapter, the candidate should be able to:

- Understand how the history of wine relates to the current state of the wine industry.
- Recognize how geography and climate affect wine production in the various countries of Europe.
- Discuss the European Union system for designating wine quality and the EU labeling laws.

EXERCISE 1: LEGALLY DEFINED WINE REGIONS: MATCHING

Fill in the blanks by matching each of the following legally defined wine regions with its country of origin. Terms may be used more than once.

Spain   Portugal   Italy   Australia   France   Germany   South Africa   United States

1. _____ Geographical Indication

2. _____ Denominación de Origen

3. _____ Wine of Origin

4. _____ Prädikatswein

5. _____ Denominazione di Origine Controllata

6. _____ Appellation d'Origine Contrôlée

7. _____ Indicazione Geographica Tipica

8. _____ Vino de Pago

9. _____ AVA

10. _____ Vinho Regional

Fill in the blanks or give a short answer for the following statements or questions.

1. The European Union was founded in _____ as an economic initiative to help relatively

   small countries compete with larger economies in the _____.

2. Approximately _____% of the global vineyard is located in Europe.

3. According to the International Organization of Vine and Wine (OIV), what were the top three
   wine-producing countries in the world?

   _____

   _____.

4. Under the new EU framework, the highest level of wine classification available is PDO, which stands for

   _____

   _____.

5. The new EU regulations permit the continuing use of pre-existing designations of origin, as long as they
   were registered prior to

   _____.

6. The second tier of quality wine under the new EU classification system is known as PGI, which stands for

   _____

   _____.

7. If a protected place-name is used on the label of a PDO wine, _____% of the grapes
   in the wine must be from the stated region.

8. If a protected place-name is used on the label of a PGI wine, _____% of
   the grapes in the wine must be from the stated region.

9. If a PDO or PGI wine states a vintage date on the label, _____% of the
   wine must be from the stated vintage.

10. If a PDO or PGI wine uses the name of a single grape variety as its name, _____% of
    the wine must be from made from the stated variety.

1. Which year best represents the beginning of the phylloxera crisis in Europe?
   a. 1650
   b. 1720
   c. 1860
   d. 1970

2. The Judgment of Paris tasting is considered a symbolic turning point in the worldwide acceptance of the wines of _____.
   a. Bordeaux
   b. Oregon
   c. Argentina
   d. California

3. It is widely believed that the earliest examples of vinifera-based wine were produced in

   _____.
   a. North America
   b. The Andes Mountains in South America
   c. The Caucasus Mountains in western Asia
   d. The Pyrenees Mountains between France and Spain

4. Under the new EU wine categorization scheme, traditional wine classifications such as France's AOC and Italy's DOCG may continue to be used, as long as the categories were registered by which of the following dates?
   a. December 31, 2009
   b. December 31, 2011
   c. January 1, 2013
   d. January 1, 2014

5. What country uses the Wine of Origin scheme to categorize its quality wines?
   a. Australia
   b. Argentina
   c. The United States
   d. South Africa

6. In the EU, if a protected place-name is used on the label of a PDO wine, what minimum percentage of the wine must be from the stated region?
   a. 100%
   b. 95%
   c. 85%
   d. 75%

7. When did the wine competition now known as the "Judgment of Paris" take place?
   a. 1875
   b. 1926
   c. 1976
   d. 1651

8. If a wine is labeled as "Pinot Grigio della Venezie IGT," what minimum percentage of the wine must be made using Pinot Grigio grapes?
   a. 100%
   b. 95%
   c. 85%
   d. 75%

9. Brokers, importers, and exporters of wine are considered to represent which of the following portions of the wine industry?
   a. Distributors
   b. Producers
   c. Retailers
   d. Regulators

10. Which of the following represents the quality tiers used for EU wines, starting with the lowest quality tier and moving up?
    a. PDO, PGI, Wine
    b. Wine, PDO, PGI
    c. PGI, Wine, PDO
    d. Wine, PGI, PDO

46

FRANCE

LEARNING OBJECTIVES

After studying this chapter, the candidate should be able to:

- Identify the general role and position of France in the global wine industry.
- Recall the geographical location and general climate of France's major wine regions.

- Discuss the hierarchy of wine designations used in France.
- Recall which grape varieties and wine styles are associated with France's important appellations.
- Describe the classification systems of the major wine regions of France.

EXERCISE 1: INTRODUCTION TO FRENCH WINES: SHORT ANSWER/FILL IN THE BLANK

Fill in the blanks or give a short answer for the following statements or questions.

1. What French wine region was greatly impacted by the 12th century marriage of Eleanor of Aquitaine to Henry II?

   _____

2. Which French wine region, situated on the border with Germany, has a history of alternating between French and German control?

   _____

3. What term is used to refer to the elevated region located in the central portion of France?

   _____

   _____

4. What is the most widely planted white wine grape variety in France?

   _____

5. What is the most widely planted red wine grape variety in France?

   _____

6. What term is used for a basic French table wine made using 100% French grapes?

   _____

7. What is the traditional term used to designate French wines of the highest quality category?

   _____

EXERCISE 2: WINE REGIONS OF FRANCE: MAP EXERCISE

Using the map below, identify the wine regions of France.

Wine Regions (Items 1 through 13):

Burgundy
Alsace
Provence
Bordeaux
Chablis
Loire Valley
Champagne
Rhône Valley
Languedoc
Southwest France
Corsica
Beaujolais
Roussillon

Cities (Items 14 through 21):

Dijon
Strasbourg
Nice
Lyon
Marseilles
Paris
Reims
Nantes

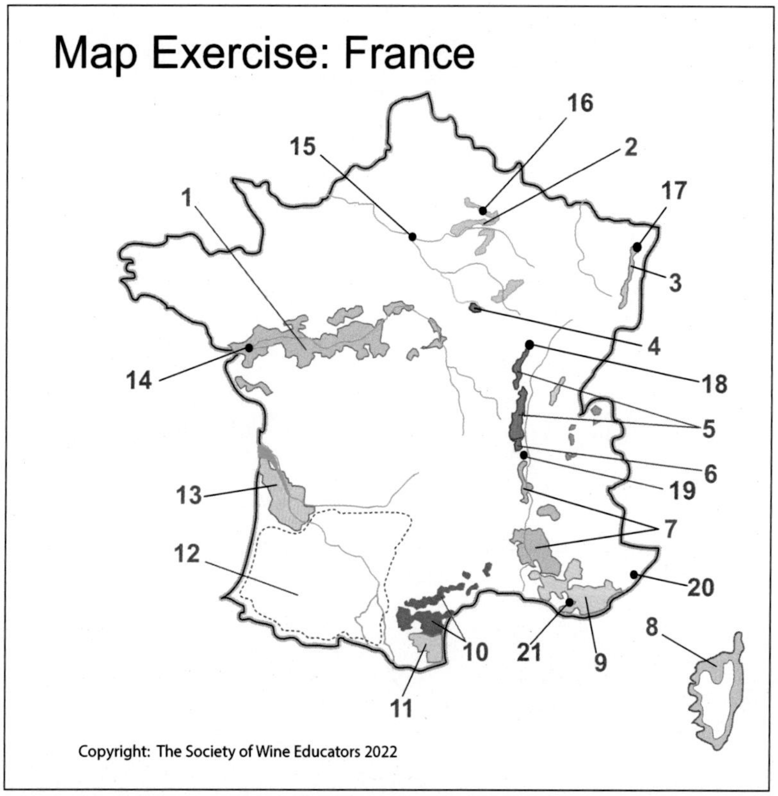
Map Exercise: France
1
2
3
4
5
6
7
8
9
10
11
12
13
14
15
16
17
18
19
20
21
Copyright: The Society of Wine Educators 2022

Figure 9-1: Map Exercise – Wine Regions of France

1. ______________________________
2. ______________________________
3. ______________________________
4. ______________________________
5. ______________________________
6. ______________________________
7. ______________________________
8. ______________________________
9. ______________________________
10. ______________________________
11. ______________________________
12. ______________________________
13. ______________________________
14. ______________________________
15. ______________________________
16. ______________________________
17. ______________________________
18. ______________________________
19. ______________________________
20. ______________________________
21. ______________________________

EXERCISE 3: BORDEAUX: MATCHING

Match each of the following terms with its appropriate definition. Each term will be used only once.

Merlot | Malbec | Garonne | Marselan
Cabernet Sauvignon | En primeur | Dordogne | Château Mouton-Rothschild
Sauvignon Blanc | Muscadelle | Gironde | Château d'Yquem
Sémillon | Cabernet Franc | Château Cheval Blanc

1. _____ The most widely planted red grape variety in the area of Entre-Deux-Mers

2. _____ Formerly a St-Émilion Premier Grand Cru Classé (category A) property

3. _____ The grape variety that forms the basis for most dry white Bordeaux wines

4. _____ A property whose ranking on the Bordeaux Classification of 1855 was changed in 1973

5. _____ Term that represents the Bordeaux tradition of selling wine in futures

6. _____ A superior first growth for sweet Bordeaux

7. _____ The grape variety that generally forms the basis for sweet Bordeaux wines such as Sauternes

8. _____ The river that flows past the city of Bordeaux and forms the border between Graves and Entre-Deux-Mers

9. _____ A minor white grape variety of Bordeaux

10. _____ The third most widely planted red grape variety in Bordeaux

11. _____ The river that flows past the city of Libourne

12. _____ The leading red grape variety of the Left Bank

13. _____ Red grape allowed for limited use in the wines of the Bordeaux AOC

14. _____ A minor red grape of Bordeaux (but one of the leading grapes of Argentina)

15. _____ An estuary that flows through the region of Bordeaux out to the Atlantic

Using the map and the terms listed below, identify the wine regions of Bordeaux.

Barsac

Margaux

Cérons

Fronsac

Graves

Saint-Émilion

Entre-Deux-Mers

Loupiac

Pessac-Léognan

Côtes de Bourg

Haut-Médoc

Pomerol

Graves de Vayres

Sainte Foy-Côtes de
Bordeaux

Sauternes

Haut-Benauge

Listrac-Médoc

Moulis-en-Médoc

Saint-Estèphe

Pauillac

Saint-Julien

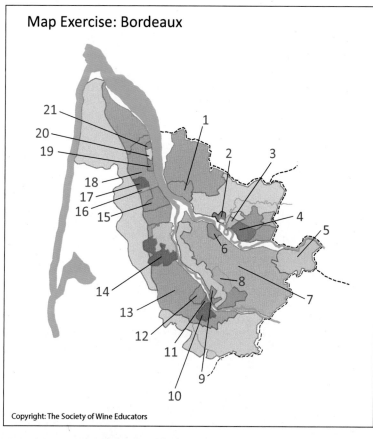

Map Exercise: Bordeaux

Copyright: The Society of Wine Educators

Figure 9-2: Map Exercise – Bordeaux

1. _____

2. _____

3. _____

4. _____

5. _____

6. _____

7. _____

8. _____

9. _____

10. _____

11. _____

12. _____

13. _____

14. _____

15. _____

16. _____

17. _____

18. _____

19. _____

20. _____

21. _____

EXERCISE 5: LEFT BANK, RIGHT BANK, OR ENTRE-DEUX-MERS?

For each of the following areas, determine whether they are located in the Left Bank, Right Bank, or Entre-Deux-Mers. Place a check mark in the correct column.

Region	Left Bank?	Right Bank?	Entre-Deux-Mers?
1. The city of Bordeaux	☐	☐	☐
2. Graves	☐	☐	☐
3. St.-Julien	☐	☐	☐
4. Fronsac	☐	☐	☐
5. Graves de Vayres	☐	☐	☐
6. Pauillac	☐	☐	☐
7. St.-Estèphe	☐	☐	☐
8. St.-Émilion	☐	☐	☐
9. Pessac-Léognan	☐	☐	☐
10. The Libournais	☐	☐	☐
11. The Médoc	☐	☐	☐
12. Pomerol	☐	☐	☐
13. Castillon-Côtes de Bordeaux	☐	☐	☐
14. Loupiac	☐	☐	☐

EXERCISE 6: THE LOIRE VALLEY: MAP EXERCISE

Using the map below, identify the following subregions and appellations of the Loire.

Touraine   Chinon   Pays Nantais   Bourgueil
Pouilly-Fumé   Anjou-Saumur   Upper Loire
Savennières   Vouvray   Sancerre

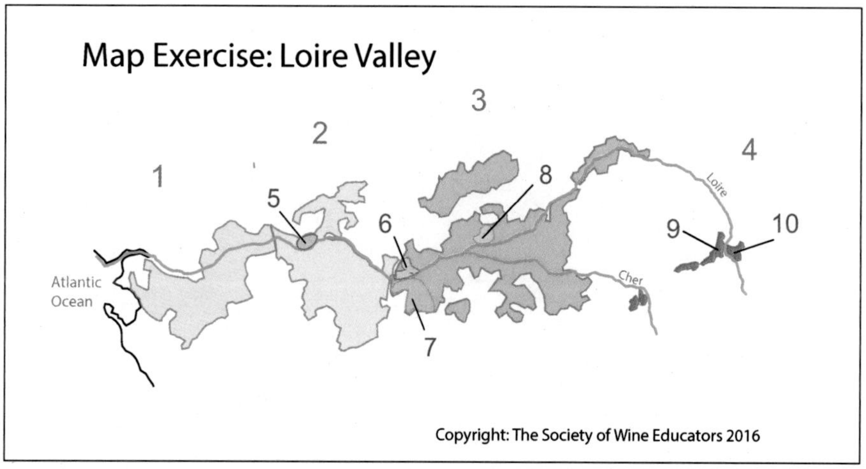

1. _____

2. _____

3. _____

4. _____

5. _____

6. _____

7. _____

8. _____

9. _____

10. _____

Map Exercise: Loire Valley

Copyright: The Society of Wine Educators 2016

Figure 9-3: Map Exercise – Loire Valley

EXERCISE 7: THE LOIRE VALLEY: KEY WHITE GRAPES

Place each of the following wine regions in the appropriate column based on the main white grape variety used in each area.

Reuilly   Bonnezeaux   Montlouis-sur-Loire   Muscadet
Pays Nantais   Menetou-Salon   Sancerre   Quarts de Chaume
Savennières   Vouvray   Pouilly-Fumé   Quincy

Sauvignon Blanc	Chenin Blanc	Melon de Bourgogne
_____	_____	_____
_____	_____	_____
_____	_____	_____
_____	_____	_____
_____	_____	_____
_____	_____	_____
_____	_____	_____

Fill in the blanks or give a short answer for the following statements or questions.

1. Of the four appellations for Muscadet, which is responsible for more than 80% of total production?

   _____

2. What winemaking procedure is often used in the Pays Nantais to make the Melon de Bourgogne-based wines taste richer and more complex?

   _____

3. What is the main grape variety used in the red wines of Chinon? _____

4. What is the main grape variety used in the red wines of Sancerre? _____

5. What marketing term is often used for the sparkling wines of the Loire? _____

   _____

6. Name three Anjou wine appellations that are known for sweet white wines:

   _____

   _____

7. What wine is the first (and only) grand cru of the Loire? _____

   _____

8. Put the following wines in order of typical sweetness, from driest to sweetest: Rosé d'Anjou, Cabernet d'Anjou, Rosé de Loire.

   _____

9. What Loire Valley white wine is often called "the most cerebral wine in the world"?

   _____

10. What is another name for Pineau de la Loire? _____

11. What grape variety goes by the name Côt? _____

12. What grape variety goes by the name Breton? _____

13. What are the three leading red wine appellations of Touraine?

   _____

Fill in the blanks or give a short answer for the following statements or questions.

1. Name the five main zones that make up the Champagne appellation: _____

   _____

   _____

2. What is the name of the chalky soil that underlies much of the Côte des Bar? _____

   _____

3. Name the three main grape varieties grown in the Champagne region: _____

   _____

4. Name the five minor grape varieties grown in the Champagne region: _____

   _____

5. What term is used to describe the juice used in the highest-quality sparkling wines?

   _____

6. What term is used to describe the juice (often used in demi-sec and extra-dry sparkling wines) from the second set of pressings?

   _____

7. What terms are used to describe the remaining juice that may be used to produce still wines or other products?

   _____

8. What is Voltis? _____

   _____

9. What term may be found on the label of a grower Champagne? _____

   _____

10. What types of wine are produced in the Coteaux Champenois AOC? _____

    _____

11. What AOC covers rosé wines produced in the far south end of the Champagne region? _____

    _____

Mark each of the following statements as true or false.

1. _____ Alsace is located across the Rhine River from the German wine region of Baden and south of the Pfalz.

2. _____ Alsace is primarily white grape territory, with Pinot Noir and Cabernet Franc being the only red grape varieties permitted in the AOC wines of the region.

3. _____ There are four types of appellations in Alsace: Alsace AOC, Alsace Premier Cru AOC, Alsace Grand Cru AOC, and Crémant d'Alsace.

4. _____ The Klevener grape variety is allowed for use in Alsace AOC wines, but it may only be grown in selected areas.

5. _____ Chasselas, Auxerrois, and Pinot Gris are all permitted grape varieties for use in Alsace AOC wines.

6. _____ There are presently 65 grand cru vineyards in Alsace.

7. _____ Gewurztraminer, Muscat, Pinot Gris, and Riesling are considered to be the four "noble grapes" of Alsace.

8. _____ The majority of the Alsace Grand Cru vineyards are located in the Bas-Rhin area.

9. _____ Due to the rain shadow of the Vosges Mountains, Alsace is one of the driest parts of France.

10. _____ Pinot Noir, Pinot Gris, and Pinot Blanc are all allowed to be grown in the Alsace AOC.

11. _____ Crémant d'Alsace accounts for approximately 45% of all wine produced in Alsace.

12. _____ Blended wines are not common in Alsace, but they are permitted to be labeled using the term *Edelzwicker*.

13. _____ The term *Gentil* may be used on the label of a blended wine from Alsace provided the wine contains a minimum of 50% noble grape varieties.

14. _____ A wine from Alsace labeled with the term *Vendage Tardive* must be produced as an ultra-sweet wine.

15. _____ In 2022, the regulations of two of the Alsace Grand Cru AOCs were revised to allow for the production of red wines crafted from Pinot Noir.

EXERCISE 11: BURGUNDY: MAP EXERCISE

Using the map and the terms listed below, identify the following wine areas and towns of Burgundy.

Côte de Beaune   Hautes-Côtes de Beaune   Nuits-Saint-Georges   Hautes-Côtes de Nuits
Tournus   Mâconnais   Côte Chalonnaise   Chablis
Côte de Nuits   Dijon   Beaune   Mâcon

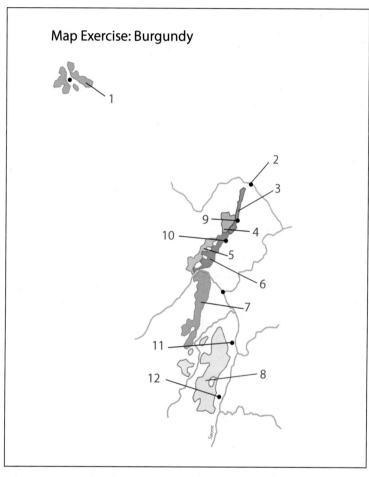

Map Exercise: Burgundy

1. _____

2. _____

3. _____

4. _____

5. _____

6. _____

7. _____

8. _____

9. _____

10. _____

11. _____

12. _____

Figure 9-4: Map Exercise – Burgundy

Match the following numbers with the descriptive statements below. Each number may be used more than once.

7	17	33	90	254
8	24	60	103	
14	32	80	129	

	Number	Definition
1.		Number of acres in the Chablis Grand Cru vineyard
2.		Percentage of Côte de Nuits production that is Pinot Noir
3.		Approximate number of miles from Chablis to the Côte d'Or
4.		Number of grand cru vineyards in the Côte de Nuits
5.		Percentage of Burgundy's annual output that is Chardonnay
6.		Number of sub-appellations in the (regional) Bourgogne AOC
7.		Number of grand cru vineyards in the Côte d'Or
8.		Total number of Burgundy grand cru vineyards
9.		Number of principal premier cru vineyards in Chablis
10.		Number of grand cru vineyards in the Côte de Beaune
11.		Number of hectares in the Chablis Grand Cru vineyard
12.		Approximate number of kilometers from Chablis to the Côte d'Or
13.		Number of grand cru vineyards in the Côte de Beaune that produce white wine only

EXERCISE 13: CÔTE DE NUITS: MAP EXERCISE

Using the map and the terms listed below, identify the following communes of the Côte de Nuits.

Vougeot

Chambolle-Musigny

Nuits-Saint-Georges

Brochon

Morey-Saint-Denis

Marsannay

Flagey-Échezeaux

Vosne-Romanée

Corgoloin

Fixin

Gevry-Chambertin

Comblanchien

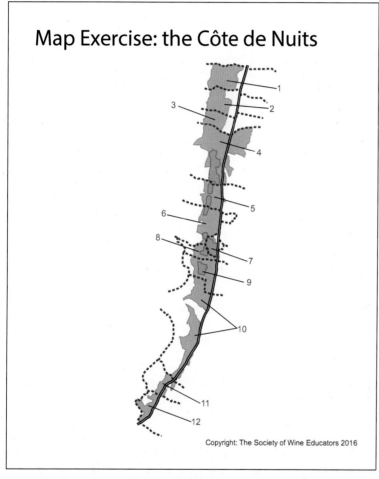

1. _____

2. _____

3. _____

4. _____

5. _____

6. _____

7. _____

8. _____

9. _____

10. _____

11. _____

12. _____

Figure 9-5: Map Exercise – Côte de Nuits

Match each of the following terms with its appropriate definition. Each term will be used only once.

Corton   Clos de Vougeot   Climat   Mercurey
Côte de Nuits   Aligoté   Grand cru   La Tâche
Montrachet   Marsannay   Côte de Beaune   Pinot Noir
Chardonnay   Gamay   Premier cru

1. _____ Minor red grape variety of Burgundy; grown primarily in the Mâconnais

2. _____ Area located in the northern end of the Côte d'Or

3. _____ Term used in Burgundy to refer to officially designated small plots of land

4. _____ The largest communal AOC located in the Côte Chalonnaise

5. _____ Commune appellation located in the Côte de Nuits

6. _____ White grape variety used in the wines of the Bouzeron AOC

7. _____ Area located on the southern end of the Côte d'Or

8. _____ Grape variety used in Pouilly-Fuissé and St.-Véran

9. _____ Highest ranking awarded to designated vineyards in Burgundy

10. _____ Grand cru vineyard with over 80 individual owners

11. _____ The only grand cru vineyard located in the Côte de Beaune that produces both red and white wine

12. _____ The main grape variety of the Côte de Nuits

13. _____ Second highest ranking awarded to designated vineyards in Burgundy

14. _____ Grand cru vineyard in the Côte de Beaune that produces white wine only

15. _____ Grand cru vineyard located in the commune of Vosne-Romanée

Using the map and the terms listed below, identify the following wine areas of the Côte de Beaune.

Saint-Romain   Chorey-lès-Beaune   Pernand-Vergelesses   Aloxe-Corton

Meursault   Volnay   Beaune   Savigny-lès-Beaune

Pommard   Puligny-Montrachet   Chassagne-Montrachet   Monthélie

Saint-Aubin   Auxey-Duresses   Santenay

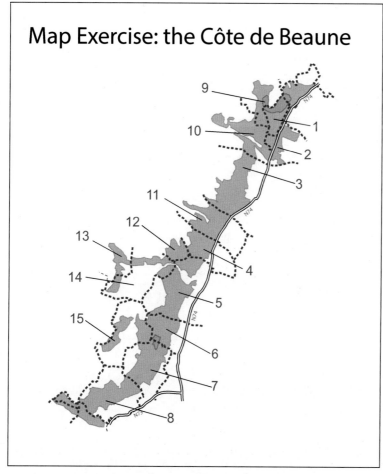

Figure 9-6: Map Exercise – Côte de Beaune

1. _____

2. _____

3. _____

4. _____

5. _____

6. _____

7. _____

8. _____

9. _____

10. _____

11. _____

12. _____

13. _____

14. _____

15. _____

EXERCISE 16: BURGUNDY: TRUE OR FALSE

Mark each of the following statements as true or false.

1. _____ Two grand cru vineyards are located in the Côte Chalonnaise.

2. _____ Due to the influence of the French Revolution and the Napoleonic Code, many vineyards in Burgundy have multiple owners.

3. _____ The Mâconnais lies directly north of Beaujolais.

4. _____ Only 10% of the total production of the Côte de Beaune is red wine.

5. _____ The name of the commune is generally listed first on the label of a Burgundy Premier Cru.

6. _____ The Mâcon-Villages AOC appellation is only designated for white wine.

7. _____ Burgundy is larger in area and produces more wine than Bordeaux.

8. _____ The weather in Chablis, with cold winters and cool summers, often makes it difficult to fully ripen grapes.

9. _____ Burgundy grands crus often use the term "1er Cru" on the label.

10. _____ Santenay is the largest communal AOC in the Côte Chalonnaise.

11. _____ Négociant trade represents about three-quarters of Burgundy's annual wine output.

12. _____ Chardonnay is the only grape variety permitted to be used in Chablis.

13. _____ All of the grand cru vineyards in the Côte de Nuits make red wine exclusively, with the exception of Musigny, which also produces a small amount of white.

14. _____ Fourchaume is a well-known Chablis Premier Cru vineyard.

15. _____ While primarily known for dry, still wines, Burgundy also produces a small amount of sparkling wine.

16. _____ Sauvignon Blanc is not approved for use in any of the AOC wines of Burgundy.

EXERCISE 17: GRAND CRU VINEYARDS OF BURGUNDY

The following chart lists some of the most famous of Burgundy's Grand Cru AOCs. For each appellation, state the commune(s) in which it is located, and whether it is approved for the production of red wine, white wine, or both. The first row has been filled in as an example.

	Grand Cru (AOC)	Commune(s)	Red, White, or Both?
1.	Montrachet	Puligny-Montrachet and Chassagne-Montrachet	White
2.	La Grande Rue		
3.	Bonnes Mares		
4.	Romanée-Conti		
5.	Clos de la Roche		
6.	Corton		
7.	Musigny		
8.	Richebourg		
9.	Échezeaux		
10.	Corton-Charlemagne		
11.	Clos de Vougeot		
12.	La Tâche		
13.	Chambertin		

Using the map and the terms listed below, identify the wine areas of Beaujolais.

Régnié	Morgon	Moulin-à-Vent	Beaujolais AOC
Chénas	Côte de Brouilly	Chiroubles	Saint-Amour
Brouilly	Juliénas	Beaujolais-Villages	Fleurie

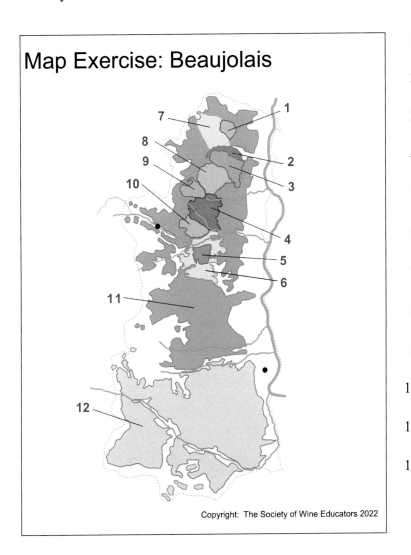

Map Exercise: Beaujolais

Copyright: The Society of Wine Educators 2022

1. _____

2. _____

3. _____

4. _____

5. _____

6. _____

7. _____

8. _____

9. _____

10. _____

11. _____

12. _____

Figure 9-7: Map Exercise – Beaujolais

Fill in the blanks or give a short answer for the following statements or questions.

1. The northern portion of the Beaujolais AOC is known for its _____ soils, which have proven ideal for the _____ grape variety.

2. The Beaujolais AOC is located to the west of the _____ River.

3. Some styles of Beaujolais have bright red and tropical fruit flavors, which may be the result of the _____ fermentation process that is often used in the region.

4. Beaujolais Nouveau is released every year on the third _____ of _____.

5. The boundaries of the Beaujolais region actually overlap slightly with those of the _____ region.

6. While the majority of the grapes grown in Beaujolais are Gamay, other grapes planted in the region include:
   _____
   _____.

7. There are a total of _____ villages in Beaujolais that are allowed to produce wines labeled with the term "Beaujolais-Villages AOC."

8. Name the three Beaujolais crus that are known for producing lighter styles of the wine:
   _____
   _____

9. Name the four Beaujolais crus that are known for producing medium- to fuller-bodied styles of the wine:
   _____
   _____

10. Name the three Beaujolais crus that are known for creating age-worthy styles of the wine:
   _____
   _____

Using the map and the terms listed below, identify the wine areas of the Rhône Valley.

Vacqueyras	Côte-Rôtie	Luberon	Beaumes-de-Venise
Ventoux	Grignan-les-Adhémar	Saint-Péray	Condrieu
Hermitage	Rasteau	Châteauneuf-du-Pape	Saint-Joseph
Château-Grillet	Cornas	Vinsobres	Tavel
Lirac	Gigondas	Crozes-Hermitage	Cairanne

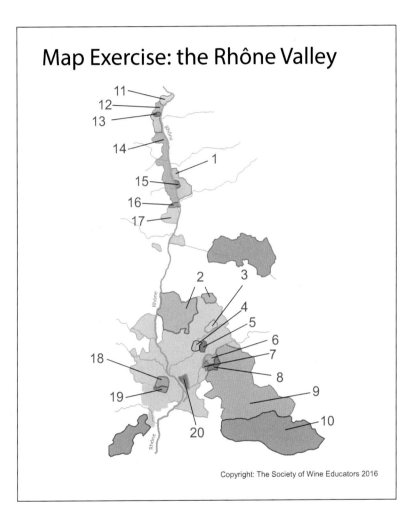

Figure 9-8: Map Exercise – The Rhône Valley

1. _____

2. _____

3. _____

4. _____

5. _____

6. _____

7. _____

8. _____

9. _____

10. _____

11. _____

12. _____

13. _____

14. _____

15. _____

16. _____

17. _____

18. _____

19. _____

20. _____

Match each of the following terms with its appropriate definition. Each term will be used only once.

Côte Rotie	Syrah	St.-Joseph	Marsanne
Tavel	Grenache	Rasteau	Clairette
Galet	Cornas	Viognier	
Mistral	Château Grillet	Grenache Blanc	

1. _____ The dominant white grape variety of the southern Rhône

2. _____ Small AOC located within the larger Condrieu AOC

3. _____ Region known for producing red vin doux naturel based on Grenache

4. _____ A rounded stone that covers the ground in some parts of the Rhône Valley

5. _____ White grape variety used to make sparkling wines with the Méthode Ancestrale Dioise

6. _____ An AOC in the northern Rhône that requires wines to be 100% Syrah

7. _____ The strong, cold wind of the Rhône and surrounding regions

8. _____ One of the larger red wine AOCs of the Northern Rhône Valley

9. _____ A white grape variety that is used, in small amounts, in the red wines of Hermitage and some of the surrounding areas

10. _____ An AOC in the southern Rhône that produces rosé exclusively

11. _____ The main red grape variety of the northern Rhône

12. _____ The northernmost appellation in the Northern Rhône Valley

13. _____ The grape variety used in Condrieu

14. _____ The main red grape variety of the southern Rhône

Using the map and the terms listed below, identify the wine areas of the Languedoc-Roussillon region.

Muscat de Saint-Jean-de-Minervois
Malepère
Minervois
Quatourze
Faugères
Muscat de Mireval
Saint-Chinian
Limoux

Cabrières
Maury
Fitou
Muscat de Frontignan
La Clape
Rivesaltes
Banyuls
St.-Georges d'Orques

Clairette du Languedoc
Cabardès
Pic Saint-Loup
Gres de Montpellier
Picpoul de Pinet
Terrasses du Larzac
Corbières

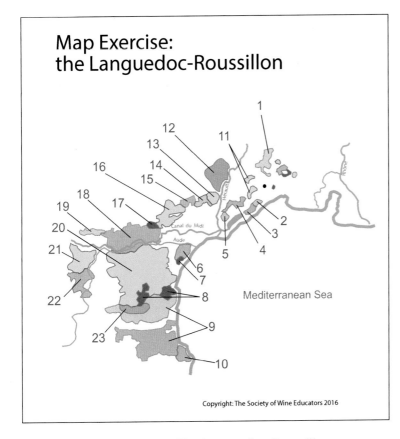

Figure 9-9: Map Exercise – The Languedoc-Roussillon

1. _____

2. _____

3. _____

4. _____

5. _____

6. _____

7. _____

8. _____

9. _____

10. _____

11. _____

12. _____

13. _____

14. _____

15. _____

16. _____

17. _____

18. _____

19. _____

20. _____

21. _____

22. _____

23. _____

Match each of the following terms with its appropriate definition. Each term will be used only once.

Bandol   Cahors   Madiran   Corbières
Fitou   Terrasses du Larzac   Limoux   Nielluccio
Côtes de Provence Rivesaltes   Arrufiac   Rolle
Fer Servadou   Sainte-Victoire

1. _____   AOC in Southwest France that produces red wines based on the Malbec grape variety

2. _____   Large AOC within Provence, well-known for rosé production

3. _____   White grape variety grown in Southwest France

4. _____   AOC in Provence known for deep reds and hearty rosés based on the Mourvèdre grape variety

5. _____   Area in the Languedoc-Roussillon known for sparkling wines

6. _____   Red grape variety grown in Southwest France

7. _____   AOC in the Languedoc approved in July of 2014

8. _____   Along with Minervois, this is one of the largest-producing AOCs of the Languedoc

9. _____   AOC in Southwest France that produces red wines based on the Tannat grape variety

10. _____   One of the oldest AOCs in the Languedoc, dating to 1948

11. _____   Sub-appellation of the Côtes de Provence AOC

12. _____   Area in the Roussillon known for fortified wines made with the Muscat grape variety

13. _____   White grape variety used in the Vin du Corse AOC; also known as Vermentino

14. _____   Red grape variety closely related to Sangiovese, used in the Vin de Corse AOC

1. Which of the following wines is produced using Sauvignon Blanc?
   a. Muscadet
   b. Vouvray
   c. Fleurie
   d. Sancerre

2. Which of the following regions, known for white wines, is located in the northern section of Graves?
   a. Fronsac
   b. Bourgueil
   c. Pessac-Léognan
   d. Vallée de la Marne

3. Which of the following grape varieties are all part of the red Bordeaux blend?
   a. Cabernet Sauvignon, Cabernet Franc, Malbec, Merlot, and Petit Verdot
   b. Cabernet Sauvignon, Cabernet Franc, Malbec, Merlot, and Pinot Noir
   c. Cabernet Sauvignon, Ruby Franc, Malbec, Merlot, and Petit Verdot
   d. Cabernet Sauvignon, Cabernet Franc, Malbec, Syrah, and Petit Verdot

4. Which of the following is the highest-quality appellation of Chablis?
   a. Chablis Premier Cru
   b. Chablis Grand Cru
   c. Chablis Cru Classé
   d. Chablis Premier Grand Cru

5. Which of the following areas is located just *south* of the Côte de Beaune?
   a. The Côte de Nuits
   b. The Côte Chalonnaise
   c. The Mâconnais
   d. Beaujolais

6. Which of the following regions produces Muscadet?
   a. Anjou-Saumur
   b. Touraine
   c. The Upper Loire
   d. The Pays Nantais

7. What is the dominant red grape variety of the southern Rhône Valley?
   a. Grenache
   b. Syrah
   c. Carignan
   d. Viognier

8. Which of the following communes is located farthest *north*?
   a. Gevry-Chambertin
   b. Vougeot
   c. Fixin
   d. Vosne-Romanée

9. Which of the following grape varieties is used in the production of Morgon?
   a. Pinot Noir
   b. Chardonnay
   c. Syrah
   d. Gamay

10. Which of the following is a small AOC located within the larger Condrieu AOC?
    a. Cornas
    b. Château-Grillet
    c. Lirac
    d. Rasteau

11. Which of the following AOCs produces 100% rosé wine?
    a. Tavel
    b. St.-Péray
    c. Clairette de Die
    d. Brouilly

12. Which of the following wines is made with a majority of Mourvèdre?
    a. Cahors
    b. Madiran
    c. Nuits-Saint-Georges
    d. Bandol

13. What percentage of the output of the wines of Provence is rosé?
    a. 25%
    b. 56%
    c. 90%
    d. 99%

14. Which of the following is a Beaujolais cru?
    a. Sancerre
    b. Brouilly
    c. Touraine
    d. Bourguiel

15. Which of the following is a white grape allowed for limited use in the wines of the Bordeaux AOC?
    a. Castets
    b. Viognier
    c. Albariño
    d. Chasselas

16. What term may be found on the label of a grower Champagne?
    a. Négociant manipulant
    b. Marche d'acheteur
    c. Récoltant manipulant
    d. Marque auxiliaire

17. Which of the following appellations is located on the Right Bank of Bordeaux?
    a. Fronsac
    b. Cérons
    c. Pauillac
    d. Margaux

18. Which of the following was the only château from Graves that was rated premier cru in the 1855 Classification of Bordeaux?
    a. Château Margaux
    b. Château Latour
    c. Château Montrose
    d. Château Haut-Brion

19. Which of the following grape varieties is used in the production of Montrachet?
    a. Sauvignon Blanc
    b. Chardonnay
    c. Pinot Noir
    d. Malbec

20. What are the three main grape varieties grown in Champagne?
    a. Pinot Noir, Meunier, and Chardonnay
    b. Chardonnay, Pinot Gris, and Pinot Noir
    c. Meunier, Pinot Blanc, and Chenin Blanc
    d. Chenin Blanc, Chardonnay, and Pinot Noir

21. Which of the following areas covers Southwest France?
    a. Terres du Midi IGP
    b. Comtés Rhodaniens IGP
    c. Comté Tolosan IGP
    d. Yonne IGP

22. Where is the Quarts de Chaume AOC located?
    a. Pays Nantais
    b. Anjou-Saumur
    c. Fréjus
    d. Côtes du Roussillon

ITALY

LEARNING OBJECTIVES

After studying this chapter, the candidate should be able to:
- Identify the general role and position of Italy in the global wine industry.
- Recall the physical location and general climate of Italy's major wine regions.
- Discuss the hierarchy of wine designations from vino to DOCG.
- Recall the grape varieties, wine styles, and important appellations in the Veneto, Piedmont, and Tuscany.
- Identify the major wine regions and grapes of other regions in Italy.

EXERCISE 1: ITALY – GRAPES AND GEOGRAPHY: TRUE OR FALSE

Mark each of the following statements as true or false.

1. _____ There is a considerable overall difference in climate between the cooler, northern portion of Italy and the hot, southern region.

2. _____ Very few parts of Italy are more than 75 miles from the sea.

3. _____ The Apennine Mountain Range forms most of the northern border of Italy.

4. _____ The rich valley of the Po River is a relatively flat area located in the southern section of Italy.

5. _____ Located along the northern edge of the country, the Alps help to prevent much of the chilling effect of the Arctic air masses from reaching Italy.

6. _____ The Tyrrhenian Sea is located along the western coast of Italy.

7. _____ Tuscany is located along Italy's Adriatic Coast.

8. _____ The Ionian Sea is located on Italy's southern border, along the coastlines of Apulia, Basilicata, and Calabria.

9. _____ Sangiovese is the most widely planted red grape variety in Italy.

10. _____ Trebbiano Toscano—one of the leading white grapes of Italy—is known elsewhere are Ugni Blanc.

Using the numbers 1–7 and the map and the terms listed below, identify the major cities of Italy.

Venice   Milan   Naples   Rome
Florence   Bologna   Turin

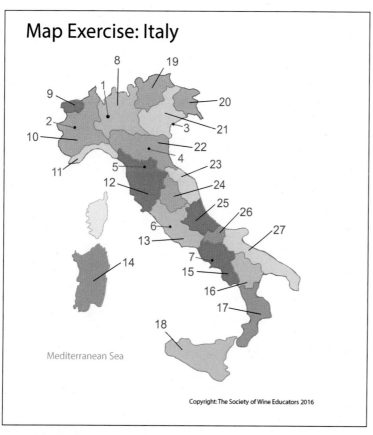

1. _____

2. _____

3. _____

4. _____

5. _____

6. _____

7. _____

Figure 10-1: Map Exercise – Italy

Using the numbers 8–27 and the map and the terms listed below, identify the major wine-producing regions of Italy.

Emilia-Romagna   Liguria   Le Marche   Molise   Basilicata
Sicily   Calabria   Tuscany   Lombardy   Piedmont
Puglia   Trentino–Alto Adige Umbria   Lazio   Abruzzo
Sardinia   Veneto   Campania   Valle d'Aosta   Friuli-Venezia Giulia

8. _____   15. _____   22. _____

9. _____   16. _____   23. _____

10. _____   17. _____   24. _____

11. _____   18. _____   25. _____

12. _____   19. _____   26. _____

13. _____   20. _____   27. _____

14. _____   21. _____

Fill in the missing information in the table below. The first row has been filled in as an example.

Appellation	Designation	Grape/Grapes	Style: Red, White, or Rosé; Dry or Sweet; Still or Sparkling
Amarone della Valpolicella	DOCG	Corvina, Corvinone, Rondinella	Red, dry, still
Recioto della Valpolicella			
Valpolicella			
Bardolino Superiore			
Bardolino Chiaretto			
Soave			
Recioto di Soave			
Asolo Prosecco			
Prosecco			

Using the map and the terms listed below, identify the major wine-producing areas of the Veneto.

Colli Berici DOC

Soave DOC

Valpolicella DOC

Colli Euganei DOC

Coneglinao Valdobbiadene Prosecco DOCG

Monti Lessini DOC

Lugana DOC

Asolo Prosecco DOCG

Custoza DOC

Breganze DOC

Lison-Pramaggiore DOC

Gambellara DOC

Vicenza DOC

Bardolino DOC

Bagnoli DOC

Piave DOC

Valdadige DOC

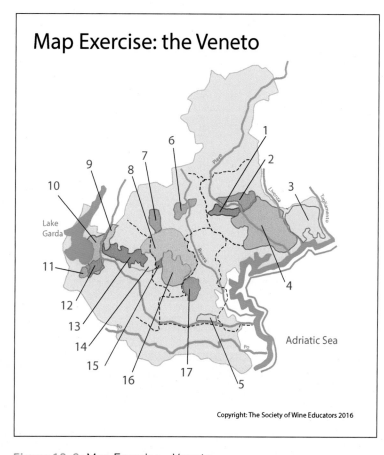

Figure 10-2: Map Exercise – Veneto

1. _____

2. _____

3. _____

4. _____

5. _____

6. _____

7. _____

8. _____

9. _____

10. _____

11. _____

12. _____

13. _____

14. _____

15. _____

16. _____

17. _____

Fill in the missing information in the table below. The first row has been filled in as an example.

Appellation	Designation	Grape/Grapes.	Style: Red, White, or Rosé; Dry or Sweet; Still or Sparkling
Barolo	DOCG	Nebbiolo	Red, dry, still
Barbaresco			
Moscato d'Asti			
Asti			
Roero			
Gattinara			
Ghemme			
Gavi			
Barbera d'Alba	'		
Acqui			

Using the map and the terms listed below, identify the major wine-producing areas of Piedmont.

Freisa di Chieri DOC   Brachetto d'Acqui DOCG   Barbaresco DOCG   Dolcetto di Ovada DOC

Gavi DOCG   Roero DOCG   Ghemme DOCG

Nizza DOCG   Gattinara DOCG   Erbaluce di Caluso DOCG

Barbera d'Asti DOCG   Barolo DOCG   Asti DOCG

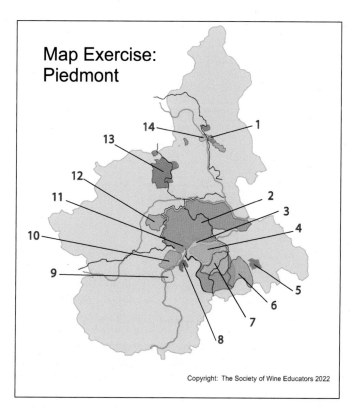

Figure 10-3: Map Exercise – Piedmont

1. _____

2. _____

3. _____

4. _____

5. _____

6. _____

7. _____

8. _____

9. _____

10. _____

11. _____

12. _____

13. _____

14. _____

Match each of the following terms with its appropriate definition. Each term will be used only once.

Appassimento	Sforzato	Valtellina	Inferno	Collio Goriziano
Südtirol	Chiavennasca	Ribolla Gialla	Spanna	Recioto
Satèn	Ripasso	Franciacorta	Metodo Classico	Langhe

1. _____ Grape variety often used in orange wines

2. _____ A winemaking process that uses partially dried grapes

3. _____ A blanc de blancs sparkling wine produced in Lombardy

4. _____ A local name for the Nebbiolo grape variety used in Lombardy

5. _____ One of the subzones of the Valtellina Superiore DOCG

6. _____ An alternative name often used for the Trentino-Alto Adige region

7. _____ A DOC, located in Friuli-Venezia Giulia, known for making white blends as well as orange wines

8. _____ A DOCG for sparkling wines from Lombardy

9. _____ Term often used in Italy to refer to the process used to create high-quality sparkling wines

10. _____ Term often used to refer to sweet wines made using grapes that are partially dried after harvest

11. _____ A local name for the Nebbiolo grape variety used in some parts of Piedmont

12. _____ A high-alcohol wine made using partially dried Nebbiolo grapes

13. _____ A region in Lombardy known for producing red wines using the Nebbiolo grape variety

14. _____ A traditional wine production technique that uses the sediment or lees from a previous batch in order to make a full-bodied wine

15. _____ A large DOC in Piedmont that covers many of the smaller regions, including Barolo, Barbaresco, and Roero

Fill in the blanks or give a short answer for the following statements or questions.

1. What are the three main cities of Tuscany? _____

   _____

2. Red wine makes up what percentage of the total output of Tuscan wine? _____

3. What term was created in response to the fact that 100% Sangiovese wines made in the Chianti region once had to be categorized as vino da tavola? _____

4. Basic Chianti DOCG must contain a minimum of _____ percent Sangiovese.

5. In addition to Sangiovese, what grapes are permitted to be used in basic Chianti?

   _____

   _____

6. What are the seven subzones of the Chianti DOCG? _____

   _____

   _____

   _____

7. Chianti Classico DOCG must contain a minimum of _____ percent Sangiovese.

8. What classification was approved by the Chianti Classico Consortium in 2014 for use with high-quality wines produced exclusively from estate-grown grapes?

   _____

9. Brunello di Montalcino DOCG must be aged for a minimum of _____ in wood and a minimum of _____ in the bottle. In addition, it may not be released before _____

   _____

10. Vin santo that is light red or amber in hue is sometimes referred to as _____

11. What is Tuscany's only white wine DOCG? _____

EXERCISE 9: TUSCANY: MATCHING

Match each of the following terms with its appropriate definition. Each term will be used only once.

Sangiovese   Governo   Tignanello   Morellino   Bolgheri
Canaiolo Nero   Vin Santo   Chianti Classico   Carmignano
Colorino   Sassicaia   Vino Nobile   Prugnolo Gentile

1. _____ The original Super Tuscan, produced by Tenuta San Guido

2. _____ Tuscan wine produced in and around the village of Montepulciano

3. _____ A Tuscan wine that must be produced using 10% to 20% Cabernet Sauvignon or Cabernet Franc

4. _____ The major red grape variety of Tuscany

5. _____ The term used for the Sangiovese grape variety in the region of Scansano

6. _____ An ancient winemaking technique that involves the addition of overripe grapes to a vat of new wine as it is finishing fermentation

7. _____ The historic heart of the Chianti region, dating back to the Middle Ages

8. _____ A type of sweet wine made in Tuscany (and other areas) using dried grapes and extensive aging

9. _____ Local name for the Sangiovese grape variety as it is used in Rosso di Montepulciano

10. _____ A red grape variety noted for its rich color and hearty tannins

11. _____ The town known as the birthplace of the Super Tuscan movement

12. _____ A red grape variety used widely throughout Tuscany as a blending partner for Sangiovese

13. _____ One of the earliest Super Tuscan-style wines, created by Marchese Piero Antinori

Using the map and the terms listed below, identify the wine-producing regions and cities in the Chianti region.

Colli Senesi	Pisa	Siena	Colli Aretini
Montespertoli	Greve	Colline Pisane	Montalbano
Chianti Classico	Florence	Colli Fiorentini	Rufina

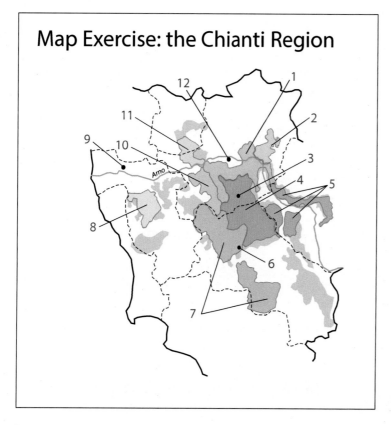

Figure 10-4: Map Exercise – Chianti

1. _____

2. _____

3. _____

4. _____

5. _____

6. _____

7. _____

8. _____

9. _____

10. _____

11. _____

12. _____

EXERCISE 11: CENTRAL ITALY: TRUE OR FALSE

Mark each of the following statements as true or false.

1. _____ Emilia-Romagna is a triangular-shaped region that stretches across the Italian Peninsula almost from one side to the other.

2. _____ Est! Est!! Est!!! is a well-known wine produced in Umbria.

3. _____ Romagna Albana DOCG (previously known as Albana di Romagna) was the first white wine to achieve the DOCG designation.

4. _____ Montepulciano d'Abruzzo DOC wines are made using a minimum of 85% Montepulciano grapes.

5. _____ Orvieto DOC is one of the leading white wines of Umbria.

6. _____ Frascati DOC is a red wine produced in the Lazio region.

7. _____ Torgiano Rosso Riserva is a DOCG wine produced in Modena.

8. _____ Castelli di Jesi Verdicchio Riserva DOCG is a crisp, dry white wine produced in the Marches region.

9. _____ Cònero DOCG, a red wine made using the Montepulciano and Sangiovese grape varieties, is produced in the Marches region.

10. _____ Most Lambrusco is produced in Emilia-Romagna; however, some is produced in Lombardy as well.

11. _____ Trebbiano d'Abruzzo is the leading red wine of the Abruzzo region.

12. _____ Orvieto DOC is based (in part) on the Trebbiano Toscano grape, locally known as Procanico.

13. _____ Cerasuolo d'Abruzzo DOC is a cherry-colored, lighter style of Montepulciano d'Abruzzo.

14. _____ Montefalco Sagrantino, made with 100% Sagrantino grapes, is a white wine produced in Umbria.

15. _____ There are four DOCs specifically for vin santo in Tuscany, including the Vin Santo del Chianti DOC.

Match each of the following terms with its appropriate definition. Each term will be used only once.

Taurasi	Sicily	Nero d'Avola	Primitivo
Negroamaro	Aglianico	Greco di Bianco	Grenache
Calabria	Campania	Fiano	
Vermentino di Gallura	Cerasuolo di Vittoria	Cirò	

1. _____ The only DOCG wine produced in Sicily

2. _____ White wine grape used in a DOCG wine of Avellino

3. _____ Region that can be described as the "toe of the boot" on Italy's peninsula

4. _____ Red grape variety used to produce a sweet, late-harvest DOCG wine in Manduria (Puglia)

5. _____ A boldly-flavored red DOCG wine produced in Campania

6. _____ DOC wine of Calabria; the red version is produced using the Gaglioppo grape variety

7. _____ Red grape variety used in the wines of the Salice Salentino DOC

8. _____ Dried-grape dessert wine produced in small amounts in Calabria

9. _____ Main grape variety used in the wines of the Cannonau di Sardegna DOC

10. _____ DOCG white wine produced on the island of Sardinia

11. _____ Island located just west of Calabria

12. _____ Main grape variety used in Cerasuolo di Vittoria

13. _____ Main grape variety used in Taurasi DOCG

14. _____ Wine region surrounding the town of Naples

Fill in the missing information regarding Marsala in the table below.

Marsala DOC	
Location	
Main Grape Varieties	
Three Main Types	

Sweetness Levels:	
Secco (dry)	
Semisecco (semidry)	
Dolce (sweet)	

Aging Requirements:	
Marsala Fine	
Marsala Superiore	
Marsala Superiore Riserva	
Marsala Vergine/Marsala Solera	
Marsala Vergine Stravecchio	

1. Which of the following is a white wine produced in Tuscany?
   a. Vernaccia di San Gimignano
   b. Morellino di Scansano
   c. Roero Arneis
   d. Orvieto

2. Which of the following grape varieties is used in the production of Gavi?
   a. Trebbiano Toscano
   b. Cortese
   c. Sangiovese
   d. Barbera

3. Which of the following terms was coined in the 1970s as a result of the strict Chianti DOC regulations in place at the time?
   a. Vin Santo
   b. Chianti Classico
   c. Super Tuscan
   d. Chianti Rufina

4. Which of the following wines is required to contain 10% to 20% Cabernet Sauvignon or Cabernet Franc?
   a. Vino Nobile di Montepulciano
   b. Super Tuscan
   c. Morellino di Scansano
   d. Carmignano

5. Chianti Classico must contain a minimum of _____ Sangiovese.
   a. 65%
   b. 75%
   c. 80%
   d. 85%

6. Which of the following phrases best describes Recioto di Soave?
   a. A dry white wine produced in Piedmont
   b. A sweet white wine produced in Piedmont
   c. A dry white wine produced in Veneto
   d. A sweet white wine produced in Veneto

7. Which of the following types of wines is produced in the DOCG surrounding the town of Asolo?
   a. Prosecco
   b. Bardolino
   c. Picolit
   d. Franciacorta

8. Which of the following wines is based on the Montepulciano grape variety?
   a. Sforzato
   b. Torgiano
   c. Cerasuolo d'Abruzzo
   d. Rosso di Montalcino

9. Which of the following wines must be made from 100% Nebbiolo grapes?
   a. Barolo and Barbaresco
   b. Barolo and Gattinara
   c. Barbaresco and Ghemme
   d. Barbaresco and Gattinara

10. Which of the following is a lightly sparkling wine produced in Piedmont?
    a. Prosecco
    b. Brachetto d'Acqui
    c. Grecco Bianco
    d. Fiano d'Avellino

11. Which of the following wines is made using the Aglianico grape variety?
    a. Rosso Conero
    b. Montefalco Sagrantino
    c. Taurasi
    d. Cannonau di Sardegna

12. Where is Marsala produced?
    a. Tuscany
    b. Sicily
    c. Umbria
    d. Calabria

13. Which of the following wine regions surrounds the city of Naples?
    a. Apulia
    b. Basilicata
    c. Calabria
    d. Campania

14. Which of the following is an alternative name often used for the Trentino-Alto Adige region?
    a. Suvereto
    b. Pavese
    c. Südtirol
    d. Cornia

15. Which of the following was the first white wine to achieve DOCG status in Italy?
    a. Romagna Albana
    b. Vermentino di Gallura
    c. Recioto di Soave
    d. Rosso Piceno

16. Castelli di Jesi Verdicchio Riserva DOCG is produced in which of the following regions?
    a. Campania
    b. Lazio
    c. Marches
    d. Lombardy

17. What are the main grape varieties used in the production of Orvieto?
    a. Sangiovese and Barbera
    b. Trebbiano Toscano and Grechetto
    c. Garganega and Sagrantino
    d. Primitivo and Aglianico

18. Which of the following wines is produced in Emilia-Romagna?
    a. Lambrusco
    b. Carmignano
    c. Prosecco
    d. Est! Est!! Est!!! di Montefiascone

19. What grape variety is used in the production of Salice Salentino?
    a. Montepulciano
    b. Primitivo
    c. Passerina
    d. Negroamaro

20. Which of the following wines is required to be produced using 100% Sangiovese?
    a. Vino Nobile di Montepulciano DOCG
    b. Carmignano DOCG
    c. Brunello di Montalcino DOCG
    d. Morellino di Scansano DOCG

21. Which of the following areas is located furthest south?
    a. Montalbano
    b. Colline Pisane
    c. Colli Senesi
    d. Barbera d'Asti

22. Which of the following DOCs extends from the Veneto and into Friuli-Venezia Giulia?
    a. Amarone della Valpolicella
    b. Lison-Pramaggiore
    c. Piave Malanotte
    d. Friuli Colli Orientali

SPAIN

LEARNING OBJECTIVES

After studying this chapter, the candidate should be able to:

- Identify the general role and position of Spain in the global wine industry.
- Recall the physical location and general climate of Spain's major wine regions.
- Recognize the hierarchy of Spanish wine designations.

- Describe the grape varieties and wine styles of Rioja, Sherry, and Cava.
- Recall the wine regions and major grapes of Galicia, the Duero Valley, Navarra, and Catalonia.
- Discuss the differences between the fino and oloroso production methods and styles for Sherry.

EXERCISE 1: SPANISH GRAPE VARIETIES: MATCHING

Match each of the following terms with its appropriate definition. Each term will be used only once.

Tinta Roriz	Cencibel	Macabeo	Albariño
Aragonêz	Monastrell	Airén	
Tinta del País	Ull de Llebre	Garnacha	

1. _____ Synonym for the Viura grape variety

2. _____ Synonym for Tempranillo used in Ribera del Duero

3. _____ Spanish term for Grenache

4. _____ Synonym for Tempranillo used in Portugal's Douro River Valley

5. _____ Spanish term for Mourvèdre

6. _____ Main grape variety used in Rías Baixas

7. _____ Synonym for Tempranillo used in Catalonia

8. _____ The most widely planted white grape variety of Spain

9. _____ Synonym for Tempranillo used in much of Portugal

10. _____ Synonym for Tempranillo used in La Mancha

Using the map and the terms listed below, identify the following wine-producing areas of Spain.

Rías Baixas	Tarragona	Navarra	Vinos de Madrid
Jumilla	Rioja	Costers del Segre	Valdeorras
La Mancha	Yecla	Bierzo	Bullas
Jerez-Xéres-Sherry	Montilla-Moriles	Priorat	Granada
Toro	Ribeiro	Ribera del Duero	
Somontano	Cigales	Valdepeñas	
Penedès	Rueda	Málaga	

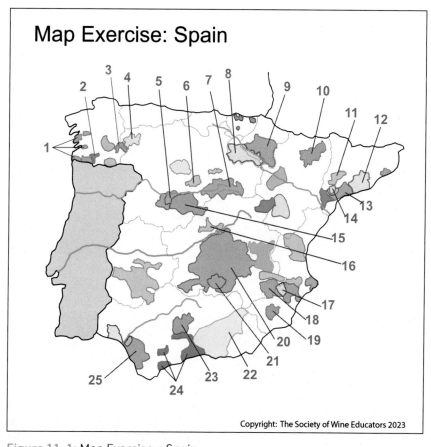

Figure 11-1: Map Exercise – Spain

Copyright: The Society of Wine Educators 2023

1. _____
2. _____
3. _____
4. _____
5. _____
6. _____
7. _____
8. _____
9. _____
10. _____
11. _____
12. _____

13. _____
14. _____
15. _____
16. _____
17. _____

18. _____
19. _____
20. _____
21. _____
22. _____

23. _____
24. _____
25. _____

EXERCISE 3: SPANISH WINE LABEL TERMS: FILL IN THE BLANK

Fill in the missing information regarding Spanish wine label laws in the table below.

Terms used by both PGI and PDO wines:	
	Wine that has spent a minimum of 18 months aging in barricas or in the bottle
	Wine that has spent a minimum of 24 months aging in barricas or in the bottle
	Wine that has spent a minimum of 36 months aging in a strongly oxidative environment and exposed to any combination of light, oxygen, and heat

Terms used by PDO wines only:				
Crianza	**Red Wines**		**White and Rosé Wines**	
	Barrel Aging:	Total Aging:	Barrel Aging:	Total Aging:
Reserva	**Red Wines**		**White and Rosé Wines**	
	Barrel Aging:	Total Aging:	Barrel Aging:	Total Aging:
Gran Reserva	**Red Wines**		**White and Rosé Wines**	
	Barrel Aging:	Total Aging:	Barrel Aging:	Total Aging:
	Term that may be used for PDO wine released the year after it was made, or aged for a shorter period of time than the minimum required for Crianza			

Match each of the following terms with its appropriate definition. Each term will be used only once.

Priorat   Navarra   Valdeorras   Cigales   Ribera del Duero
Rueda   Tarragona   Ribeiro   Galicia   Bierzo
Montsant   Somontano   Penedès   Rías Baixas

1. _____ Located just to the west of Ribera del Duero, this DO is known mainly for reds and rosados based on the Tinta del Pais and Garnacha grape varieties

2. _____ This DO is well-known as one of the first areas in Spain to modernize wine production and was the first to use stainless steel temperature-controlled fermentation

3. _____ DO located in the foothills of the Pyrenees, within the region of Aragón

4. _____ The most famous of Galicia's wine regions, known for high-acid wines made from Albariño, Loureira, and Treixadura

5. _____ Galician region known for Godello-based white wines

6. _____ A DO known for white wines based on the Verdejo grape variety

7. _____ DO—located just to the north of the Rioja DOCa—historically known for rosados (and currently expanding with international varieties)

8. _____ A Galician DO that produces white wines based on Treixadura and other local grapes

9. _____ Region known for Mencía-based red wines

10. _____ DO famous for Garnacha-based wines and llicorella soils

11. _____ A small DO, created in 2001 and located adjacent to Priorat

12. _____ Area located in the northwest corner of Spain, exposed to the Atlantic Ocean, and often referred to as part of *Green Spain*

13. _____ Region in the Duero Valley with some of the highest-elevation vineyards in Spain

14. _____ Large DO located in Catalonia, just south of Penedès

Using numbers 1–8 and the terms below, identify the main cities in the Rioja region, and the provinces in and surrounding the Rioja region.

Navarra   La Rioja   Zaragoza   Soria
Burgos   Alava   Logroño   Haro

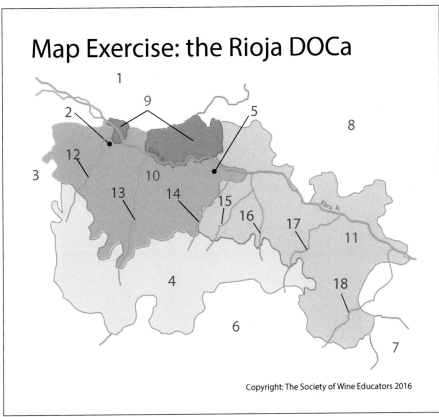

Figure 11-3: Map Exercise – the Rioja DOCa

Using numbers 9–11 and the terms below, identify the zones of the Rioja DOCa.

Rioja Oriental   Rioja Alta   Rioja Alavesa

Using numbers 12–18 and the terms below, identify the river valleys of the Rioja region.

Najerilla Valley   Cidacos Valley   Iregua Valley
Leza Valley   Alhama Valley
Jubera Valley   Oja Valley

1. _____

2. _____

3. _____

4. _____

5. _____

6. _____

7. _____

8. _____

9. _____

10. _____

11. _____

12. _____

13. _____

14. _____

15. _____

16. _____

17. _____

18. _____

Fill in the blanks for the following statements or questions.

1. In the year _____, Rioja was the first wine region in Spain to be elevated to _____ status.

2. The Rioja region lies in the _____ River Valley, mostly in the province of _____. About one-third of the vineyards are situated within the neighboring provinces of _____ and _____.

3. The _____ is the high-altitude, hilly subregion of Rioja located mainly south of the Ebro River.

4. The _____ is located on the western side of the Rioja area, north of the Ebro River.

5. The _____ is the flatter, eastern area of the Rioja.

6. Red varieties cover well over _____% of the vineyard area in Rioja.

7. _____ is the main red grape of the area, while other permitted red grapes include _____.

8. What is the principal grape variety used in white Rioja? _____.

9. Other indigenous white grapes used in white Rioja include _____. The international varieties _____ are now being planted as well.

10. Rioja's prominence is in part due to winemakers from _____ who settled in the region not long after phylloxera arrived in France.

11. Red Rioja is typically aged in barrels made of _____.

12. The long aging periods for red Rioja mean less of a focus on _____ flavors and more emphasis on _____.

13. Rioja Rosado is generally made from a blend of grapes dominated by the _____ grape variety.

14. Red Rioja DOCa using the Gran Reserva designation must age for a total of _____ months, to include a minimum of _____ months in the barrel and _____ months in the bottle.

Mark each of the following statements as true or false.

1. _____ In the 1870s, the first bottles of Cava were produced in the Catalonian town of San Sadurní de Noya (Sant Sadurní d'Anoia).

2. _____ Most Cava is produced using the Charmat method.

3. _____ All cava must be aged in the bottle, on the lees, for a minimum of 18 months.

4. _____ Nearly 95% of Cava is produced in Basque Country and Galicia.

5. _____ The three classic grape varieties for Cava are Macabeo, Xarel-lo, and Parellada.

6. _____ The three classic grape varieties for Cava are all red.

7. _____ A portion of the Cava DO is located in the Ebro Valley.

8. _____ The Viñedos de Almendralejo region is located in Galicia.

9. _____ Cava de Paraje Calificado must be lees-aged for a minimum of 36 months.

10. _____ Trepat, a white grape, is widely used in all styles of Cava.

11. _____ Pinot Noir, Garnacha, and Monastrell are allowed for use in Cava.

12. _____ Corpinnat is not a protected geographical indication; but is rather an EU-recognized brand name with its own set of standards.

13. _____ Corpinnat must be produced using international varieties such as Chardonnay, Sauvignon Blanc, and Pinot Noir.

14. _____ Corpinnat must be produced from hand-harvested grapes grown using organic farming methods.

15. _____ Any wine labeled as "Cava de Guarda" must be traceable from the vineyard to the bottle.

Match each of the following terms with its appropriate definition. Each term will be used only once.

Pale Cream	Albariza	Pedro Ximénez	Arena	Palo Cortado
Barro	Amontillado	Moscatel	Fino	Cream
Oloroso	Manzanilla	Palomino	Montilla-Moriles	

1. _____ The general category of Sherries that undergo biological aging

2. _____ General category of Sherries that do not develop flor

3. _____ A specific type of Sherry that must be aged in Sanlúcar de Barrameda

4. _____ Type of sweetened fino Sherry originally made in Bristol

5. _____ Most widely grown grape variety in the Jerez DO

6. _____ Grape variety—widely grown in the Montilla-Moriles DO—used to produce a type of dried-grape Sherry

7. _____ Local name for the Muscat of Alexandria grape variety

8. _____ White, chalky soil ideal for growing Palomino grapes

9. _____ Clay soil preferred by Pedro Ximénez grapes

10. _____ Sandy soil good for growing Moscatel grapes

11. _____ Wine region that lies to the east of Jerez, known for Sherry-style wines

12. _____ Style of Sherry—known for nutty aroma—that starts out a fino but is subsequently aged without flor

13. _____ A rare style of Sherry made from fino-quality wine that did not develop flor as expected

14. _____ A sweetened oloroso Sherry

1. Which of the following grape varieties is a major component in the wines of Rías Baixas?
   a. Albariño
   b. Macabeo
   c. Verdejo
   d. Airén

2. Which of the following represents the three subregions of the Rioja region?
   a. Rioja Alta, Rioja Baja, and Rioja del Sur
   b. Rioja Alta, Rioja Norte, and Rioja Ebro
   c. Rioja Oriental, Rioja Ebro, and Rioja Alavesa
   d. Rioja Alta, Rioja Alavesa, and Rioja Oriental

3. What are the three classic grape varieties used in the production of Cava?
   a. Macabeo, Verdejo, and Pinot Noir
   b. Parellada, Macabeo, and Verdejo
   c. Xarel-lo, Pinot Noir, and Macabeo
   d. Macabeo, Parellada, and Xarel-lo

4. Which of the following wine regions specializes in crisp white wines based on the Verdejo grape variety?
   a. Priorat
   b. Ribeira Sacra
   c. Rueda
   d. Jerez

5. What is the minimum lees aging time required for Cava de Paraje Calificado?
   a. 36 months
   b. 24 months
   c. 60 months
   d. There is no minimum

6. Which of the following wine regions is a DOCa known for its llicorella soils?
   a. Ribera del Duero
   b. Priorat
   c. Navarra
   d. Málaga

7. What is the main grape variety used in white Rioja?
   a. Palomino
   b. Garnacha Blanca
   c. Viura
   d. Malvasia

8. What is the most widely grown grape variety in Spain?
   a. Merlot
   b. Tempranillo
   c. Garnacha
   d. Macabeo

9. Which of the following areas contains more *vinos de pago* than any other region of Spain?
   a. Andalucía
   b. Galicia
   c. Castilla-La Mancha
   d. Castilla y León

10. What are the three main soils in the region of Jerez?
    a. Albariza, Barro, and Clay
    b. Barro, Arena, and Albariza
    c. Arena, Llicorella, and Barro
    d. Llicorella, Albariza, and Arena

11. Which of the following aging terms may be used for PDO wines that are released the year after harvest?
    a. Joven
    b. Tipica
    c. Pago
    d. Calificado

12. How much total aging time is required for a typical Spanish red wine labeled as a Crianza?
    a. Six months
    b. One year
    c. Eighteen months
    d. Two years

13. How does the Crianza aging requirement for red Rioja differ from that of other Spanish red wines?
    a. Red Rioja requires more time in wood than other red wines.
    b. Red Rioja requires less time in wood than other red wines.
    c. Red Rioja must spend the entire length of the required aging time in wood.
    d. Red Rioja must be fermented in new oak barrels in order to use the term "Crianza."

14. How much total aging time is required for a typical Spanish red wine labeled as a Reserva?
    a. Two years
    b. Three years
    c. Four years
    d. Five years

15. In Jumilla, the Mourvèdre grape variety is often known as _____.
    a. Tinta Roriz
    b. Ul de Llebre
    c. Macabeo
    d. Monastrell

16. Which of the following wine regions is located just to the northeast of the Rioja DOCa?
    a. Ribera del Duero
    b. Penedès
    c. Navarra
    d. Jumilla

17. The Somontano DO is located within which of the following autonomous regions?
    a. Catalonia
    b. Aragón
    c. Castilla-La Mancha
    d. La Rioja

18. What are the two leading grape varieties of the Priorato DOCa?
    a. Garnacha and Cariñena
    b. Tempranillo and Tinta Roriz
    c. Macabeo and Viura
    d. Mazuelo and Cariñena

19. What is the leading grape variety of the Bierzo DO?
    a. Tempranillo
    b. Godello
    c. Mencía
    d. Garnacha

20. Of the following, which region is best known for Treixadura-based white wine?
    a. Cigales
    b. Rueda
    c. Montsant
    d. Ribeiro

PORTUGAL

CHAPTER TWELVE

LEARNING OBJECTIVES

After studying this chapter, the candidate should be able to:

- Identify the physical location and general climate of Portugal's major wine regions.
- Recognize the hierarchy of wine designations from Vinho de Portugal to DOC.

- Describe the major grape varieties and wine styles of Port and Madeira.
- Recall significant DOCs for unfortified wine and their primary grape varieties.

EXERCISE 1: PORTUGUESE GRAPE VARIETIES: MATCHING

Match each of the following terms with its appropriate definition. Each term will be used only once.

Tinta Roriz	Gouveio	Alvarinho	Touriga Franca	Trincadeira
Baga	Fernão Pires	Malvasia	Touriga Nacional	Castelão

1. _____ One of the primary red grapes used in Port; provides firm structure and black-fruit flavors

2. _____ Red grape variety sometimes referred to as Periquita

3. _____ Portugal's most widely grown white grape variety

4. _____ White grape variety grown in the Vinho Verde region; also the star of Spain's Rías Baixas DO

5. _____ White grape variety used in a sweet style of Madeira, where it is sometimes referred to as Malmsey

6. _____ Red grape variety also known as Tempranillo

7. _____ Red grape variety also known as Tinta Amarela

8. _____ One of the predominant white grape varieties used in white Port

9. _____ One of the primary red grape varieties used in Port; lends floral notes to the blend

10. _____ Highly tannic red grape variety; often used in the red wines of the Bairrada DOC

Using the map and the terms listed below, identify the regional wine designations of Portugal.

Alentejano   Península de Setúbal   Terras do Dão   Minho
Lisboa   Beira Atlântico   Algarve   Duriense
Tejo   Transmontano   Terras da Beira   Terras de Cister

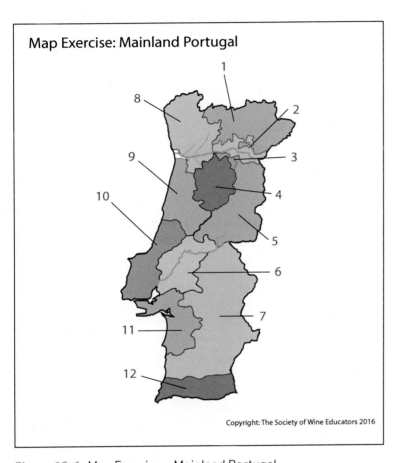

Map Exercise: Mainland Portugal

Copyright: The Society of Wine Educators 2016

Figure 12-1: Map Exercise – Mainland Portugal

1. _____

2. _____

3. _____

4. _____

5. _____

6. _____

7. _____

8. _____

9. _____

10. _____

11. _____

12. _____

Fill in the blanks or give a short answer for the following statements or questions.

1. A light, often low-alcohol wine is produced in the Minho region under the _____ DOC.

2. The two main grape varieties used in white Vinho Verde are _____

   _____.

3. Red Vinho Verde is made primarily from the _____ grape variety.

4. Unfortified wines produced in the Douro River Valley from traditional Port grape varieties are categorized as

   _____ _____.

5. Unfortified wines produced in the Douro River Valley from international grape varieties such as Cabernet Sauvignon are categorized as _____.

6. The Baga grape is used to make highly tannic red wines under the _____ DOC.

7. The _____ DOC, located just south of the Minho region, produces many styles of wine but focuses on _____.

8. The Península de Setúbal is home to a well-known, sweet wine produced from the Muscat grape, known as

   _____.

9. _____ is the southernmost Portuguese wine region on the mainland.

10. The _____ region is located on a chain of nine islands approximately 1,000 miles off the west coast of Portugal. Three islands, _____ _____ _____, have their own DOCs.

11. The _____ DOC, located along the Atlantic coastline, is well-known for its vineyards protected by sand dunes and wooden fences.

12. The _____ DOC is located within the Península de Setúbal region and produces mainly red wines based on the _____ grape variety.

EXERCISE 4: THE DOURO DOC: MAP EXERCISE

Using numbers 1–3 and the terms below, identify the three main subregions of the Douro.

Cima Corgo | Baixa Corgo | Douro Superior

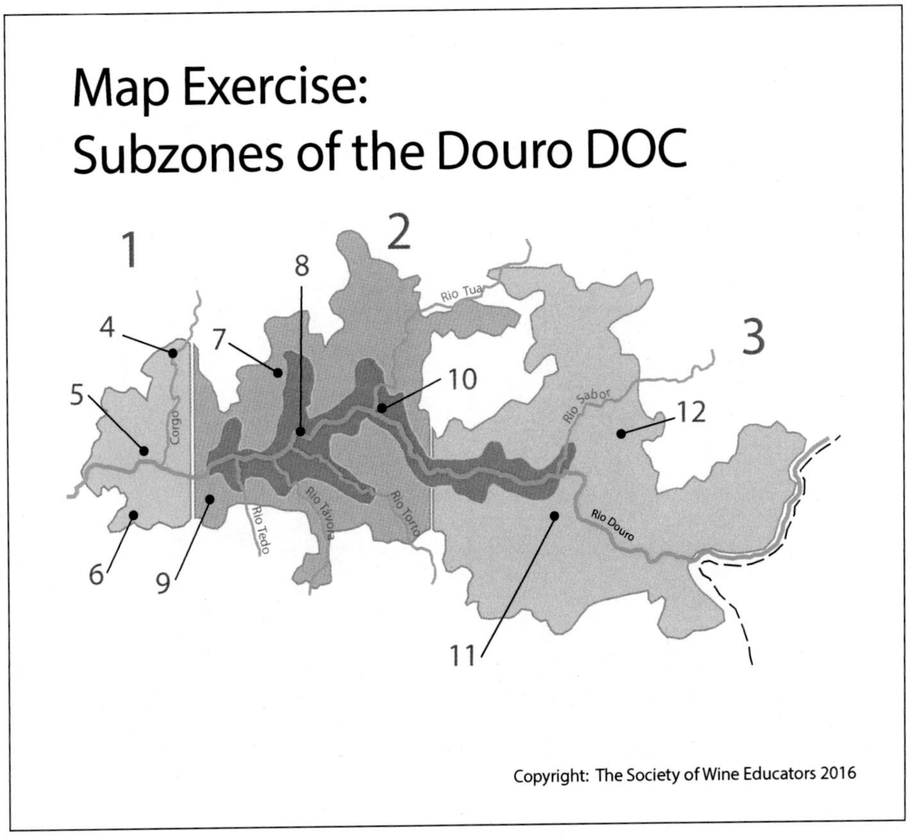

Figure 12-2: Map Exercise – Subzones of the Douro DOC

1. ____________________
2. ____________________
3. ____________________
4. ____________________
5. ____________________
6. ____________________
7. ____________________
8. ____________________
9. ____________________
10. ____________________
11. ____________________
12. ____________________

Using numbers 4–12 and the terms listed below, identify the main towns and municipalities located within the Douro.

Pinhão
Régua
Torre de Moncorvo
Sabrosa
Vila Nova de Foz Côa
Armamar
Tua
Vila Real
Lamego

Fill in the missing information regarding Port in the table below.

PORT	
Region of origin:	
Subregions:	
GRAPE VARIETIES:	
Five preferred red grape varieties:	
Two predominant white grape varieties:	
STYLES OF PORT:	
	The simplest style of Port; aged in large oak vats for about two years before being bottled and ready-to-drink
	Wine from a single year, matured in large oak casks for four to six years after harvest
	Port that has been aged in oak for a minimum of seven years before bottling
	Wine from a single year designated as being an outstanding year; aged for two to three years in cask before being bottled
	Port produced from the grapes of one year and one estate
	A single-vintage tawny Port
	Port produced using Malvasia Fina and Gouveio grapes, among others
	Non-traditional style of Port originally produced by Croft, first released in 2008

Fill in the blanks or give a short answer for the following statements or questions.

1. Madeira is produced on an island located in the _____ Ocean, approximately _____ miles/km off the coast of Morocco.

2. All fortified wine produced on the island is categorized as _____.

3. Unfortified table wines produced on the island are considered *Vinho Regional* and are categorized as _____.

4. The most widely planted grape on the island is _____.

5. The four noble grapes of Madeira are _____ _____.

6. Madeira can be made in both dry and sweet styles, depending on whether the wine is _____ _____ during fermentation or after.

7. The dry styles of Madeira are made from _____ _____ grapes.

8. The sweet styles of Madeira are made from _____ _____ grapes.

9. In the _____ method of production, Madeira is stored in the rafters of a warm building and allowed to age for several years.

10. In the _____ method of production, Madeira is left in a concrete or stainless steel vat and heated via hot water for several months.

11. The finest Madeiras are made using the _____ method.

12. The four styles of Madeira are described as:

Sercial: _____

Verdelho: _____

Boal: _____

Malmsey: _____

1. Which of the following grape varieties is known for providing Port with a firm structure and black-fruit flavors?
   a. Tinta Roriz
   b. Trincadeira
   c. Touriga Franca
   d. Touriga Nacional

2. Which of the following grape varieties is known for providing Port with floral and blackberry notes?
   a. Tinta Roriz
   b. Trincadeira
   c. Touriga Franca
   d. Touriga Nacional

3. Which of the following grape varieties is also known as Tempranillo?
   a. Baga
   b. Castelão
   c. Tinta Roriz
   d. Tinta Cão

4. Vinho Verde is produced in which of the following regions?
   a. The Minho
   b. Algarve
   c. Alentejano
   d. The Dão

5. What are the three subregions of the Douro Valley?
   a. Baixo Corgo, Baixo Superior, and Douro Baja
   b. Douro Superior, Douro Alta, and Cima Corgo
   d. Douro Duriense, Cima Corgo, and Baixo Corgo
   d. Cima Corgo, Baixo Corgo, and Douro Superior

6. Which of the following properly lists the traditional styles of Madeira, in order from driest to sweetest?
   a. Sercial, Verdelho, Boal, Malmsey
   b. Malmsey, Boal, Sercial, Verdelho
   c. Boal, Verdelho, Malmsey, Sercial
   d. Verdelho, Sercial, Boal, Malmsey

7. Which of the following styles of Port, considered to be the simplest style, is aged in large oak vats for two years before being bottled and ready-to-drink?
   a. Tawny Port
   b. Ruby Port
   c. Vintage Port
   d. Fino Port

8. Which of the following is a single-vintage tawny Port?
   a. Late-Bottled Vintage Port
   b. Primo Port
   c. Colheita Port
   d. Single Quinta Port

9. What style of Port is produced using wine from a single year, matured in large oak casks for four to six years after harvest?
   a. Vintage Port
   b. Ruby Port
   c. Colheita Port
   d. Late-Bottled Vintage Port

10. Which of the following island chains produces wine about 1,000 miles off the west coast of Portugal?
    a. The Canary Islands
    b. The Azores
    c. The Gulf Islands
    d. The Ionian Islands

11. The Baga grape variety is known for which of the following properties?
    a. High tannin
    b. Deep yellow color
    c. Low acid
    d. Being seedless

12. The region of Setúbal is known for which of the following wines?
    a. Baga de Arrábida
    b. Fernão Pires de Península
    c. Moscatel de Setúbal
    d. Lagos de Setúbal

UNIT THREE WINE LABELS, LAWS, AND REGIONS

GERMANY

LEARNING OBJECTIVES

After studying this chapter, the candidate should be able to:

- Discuss the general role and position of Germany in the global wine industry.
- Recall the physical location and general climate of Germany's major wine regions.
- Recognize the importance of Riesling to the German wine industry.

- Understand the hierarchy of wine designations from Wein to Prädikatswein, along with the progression of Prädikat levels from Kabinett to Trockenbeerenauslese.
- Discuss the differences among Anbaugebiete, Bereiche, Grosslagen, and Einzellagen.
- Identify the grape varieties and wine styles of the key wine regions of Germany.

EXERCISE 1: GERMANY: MAP EXERCISE

Using numbers 1–6 and the terms listed below, identify the following German cities.

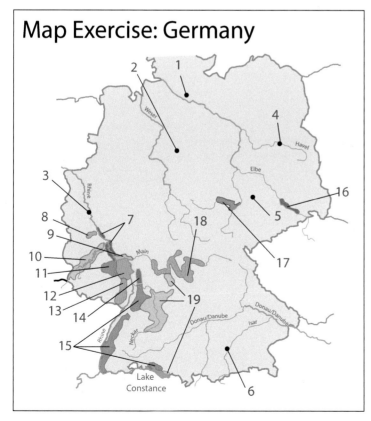

Map Exercise: Germany

Berlin	Munich	Hamburg
Hanover	Cologne	Leipzig

1. _____

2. _____

3. _____

4. _____

5. _____

6. _____

Figure 13-1: Map Exercise – Germany

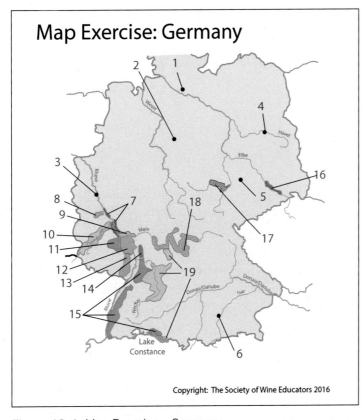

Figure 13-1: Map Exercise – Germany

7. _____

8. _____

9. _____

10. _____

11. _____

12. _____

13. _____

14. _____

15. _____

16. _____

17. _____

18. _____

19. _____

Using numbers 7–19 and the terms listed below, identify the location of the 13 main wine regions of Germany.

Rheinhessen	Franken	Saale-Unstrut
Sachsen	Nahe	Mosel
Baden	Pfalz	Hessische Bergstrasse
Württemberg	Rheingau	
Ahr	Mittelrhein	

Match each of the following terms with its appropriate definition. Each term will be used only once.

Geschützte Ursprungsbezeichnung (gU)   Halbtrocken
Edelfäule   Qualitätswein
Prädikatswein   Weissburgunder
Wein   Deutscher Wein
Geschützte Geographische Angabe (ggA)   Oechsle
Trocken   Spätburgunder
Grauburgunder   Riesling

1. _____   German name for Pinot Gris

2. _____   German name for Pinot Blanc

3. _____   Most widely planted red grape in Germany, also known as Pinot Noir

4. _____   A German table wine made from 100% German grapes

5. _____   A German table wine that may be produced from imported bulk wine

6. _____   Most widely planted grape in Germany

7. _____   German wine category that contains what used to be referred to as "Landwein"

8. _____   Term used for dry German wines

9. _____   Term used for off-dry German wines

10. _____   Term used to denote all German PDO wines

11. _____   Category of German PDO wines that allows for chaptalization

12. _____   Category of German PDO wines that does not allow chaptalization

13. _____   German term for botrytis

14. _____   Scale used to measure sugar ripeness (grape must density) in Germany

Fill in the blanks with the appropriate term for the subcategories of Prädikatswein, listed in ascending order of grape ripeness.

1. _____ The lowest ripeness level of the German Prädikat

2. _____ Wines of additional ripeness made from grapes picked after a designated date; translates as "late harvest"

3. _____ Translating as "selected harvest," these wines are made from grapes that have reached a required level of sugar

4. _____ Translating as "selected berries," these are sweet wines that may be affected by botrytis

5. _____ Wines made from frozen grapes that must be harvested at the same level of ripeness as the previous category

6. _____ Wines made from individually picked, overripe berries that are often affected by botrytis

EXERCISE 4: GEOGRAPHICAL INDICATIONS: SHORT ANSWER/FILL IN THE BLANK

Fill in the blanks with the appropriate term for the geographical indications for German wines, listed in order from largest to smallest.

1. _____ Germany has 13 of these designated wine regions.

2. _____ Equal to regional or district appellations, Germany has approximately 40 of these designated areas.

3. _____ Equivalent to a large grouping of closely located vineyards, approximately 160 of these designated areas exist in Germany.

4. _____ This area may contain a single vineyard or a small group of vineyards. There are approximately 2,700 of these areas in Germany.

Match each of the following terms with its appropriate definition. Each term will be used only once.

Verband Deutscher Prädikatsweingüter (VDP)   Feinherb   Grosses Gewächs
Lieblich   Gutsabfüllung   Abfüller
Süssreserve   Grosse Lage   Erste Lage
Weissherbst   Sekt   Trocken
Erzeugerabfüllung   Chaptalization   Schaumwein

1. _____ An organization of German wine estates committed to terroir-driven viticulture

2. _____ Term used to indicate that a wine was made from the highest-level vineyards of a VDP estate

3. _____ Term used to indicate that a wine is made from the second highest level of a VDP estate

4. _____ Unfermented grape juice that is sometimes used to increase the sweetness in a wine

5. _____ Label term used to indicate an estate-bottled wine

6. _____ Label term that indicates a producer-bottled wine made by grower cooperatives

7. _____ Label term that indicates a wine produced by a commercial winery from purchased grapes

8. _____ Label term that while legally undefined, generally refers to an off-dry wine

9. _____ Label term that indicates a semi-sweet wine

10. _____ Label term that typically refers to a wine with a sugar level of 9g/L or less

11. _____ Label term that may be used on a dry wine produced from a VDP Grosse Lage vineyard

12. _____ German sparkling wine produced via carbonation

13. _____ The practice of adding sugar to must before fermentation

14. _____ A German rosé of at least Qualitätswein quality made from a single variety

15. _____ German sparkling wine typically produced via the tank method

Match each of the following terms with its appropriate definition. Each term may be used more than once.

Baden   Sachsen   Württemberg   Rheingau   Rheinhessen
Pfalz   Ahr   Mosel   Franken

1. _____   This small area produces only 2% of Germany's wines, yet its wines enjoy an excellent reputation

2. _____   One of the wine regions located in the former East Germany

3. _____   The largest wine region of Germany in terms of both area under vine and wine production

4. _____   The largest wine region of Germany in terms of ground area; however, only a small portion of the area is planted with grapes

5. _____   Region planted to over 80% red grapes and specializing in Spätburgunder, despite being located on the 50th parallel

6. _____   Region known for slate in the topsoil, steep slopes, and excellent Riesling

7. _____   This region is home to the well-known Bereich of Johannisberg

8. _____   Wine region that lies west of the Rhine River, with its southern edge stretching almost to Alsace

9. _____   Region with the most Einzellagen (over 500)

10. _____   Region with most of its vines planted along the Neckar River and in the Neckar River Valley

11. _____   Region near the city of Wiesbaden known for red slate soils

12. _____   Region that is home to six Bereiche, including Bernkastel, Saar, and Ruwertal

13. _____   This region is sometimes referred to as Palatinate

14. _____   The regional home of the Kaiserstuhl Bereich, noted for its warm weather

15. _____   Wines from this region are often packaged in a flask-shaped Bocksbeutel

16. _____   Large region focusing on red wine, including Trollinger, Schwarzriesling (Pinot Meunier), and Lemberger

1. Which of the following grapes is known in Germany as Grauburgunder?
   a. Riesling
   b. Pinot Gris
   c. Pinot Blanc
   d. Chardonnay

2. What is the most widely planted white grape variety in Germany?
   a. Riesling
   b. Müller-Thurgau
   c. Silvaner
   d. Grauburgunder

3. What is the most widely planted red grape variety in Germany?
   a. Pinot Noir
   b. Merlot
   c. Dornfelder
   d. St. Laurent

4. Which of the following German wine regions is located in the former East Germany?
   a. Mittelrhein
   b. Pfalz
   c. Sachsen
   d. Baden

5. Which of the following German wine regions is located farthest north?
   a. Baden
   b. Württemberg
   c. Franken
   d. Ahr

6. Which of the following grapes is known in Germany as Weissburgunder?
   a. Pinot Noir
   b. Pinot Blanc
   c. Silvaner
   d. Chardonnay

7. In the context of the German wine industry, which of the following terms refers to the most specific area?
   a. Anbaugebiet
   b. Grosslage
   c. Bereich
   d. Einzellage

8. What is Sekt?
   a. An off-dry German rosé
   b. A German sparkling wine
   c. A dry white wine produced using a blend of grape varieties
   d. A term used to refer to a co-operatively run wine estate

9. Of the following list of terms, which indicates the highest level of ripeness?
   a. Beerenauslese
   b. Kabinett
   c. Spätlese
   d. Auslese

10. Which of the following terms represents the highest classification of quality German wines?
    a. ggA (geschützte geographische Angabe)
    b. Gutswein
    c. Prädikatswein
    d. Deutscher Wein

11. What scale is used in Germany to measure grape density and ripeness?
    a. Brix
    b. Feinherb
    c. Abfüller
    d. Oechsle

12. Which of the following terms is used by the members of the VDP (Verband Deutscher Prädikatsweingüter) to indicate that the wine was made from the highest-level vineyards of an estate?
    a. Grosse Lage
    b. Erste Lage
    c. Charta
    d. Selection

13. Which of the following terms is used to refer to the 13 designated wine regions in Germany?
    a. Grosslagen
    b. Anbaugebiete
    c. Einzellagen
    d. Bereiche

14. Which of the following German wine regions is the largest, both in terms of area under vine and wine production?
    a. Rheinhessen
    b. Baden
    c. Ahr
    d. Mosel

15. Which of the following German wine regions is largely planted to red grapes?
    a. Mosel
    b. Hessische Bergstrasse
    c. Württemberg
    d. Mittelrhein

16. Where is the Mittelrhein area located?
    a. Downriver (north) of the Rheingau
    b. Upriver (south) of the Pfalz
    c. East of Sachsen
    d. North of Berlin

17. Which of the following is the easternmost wine region of the former West Germany?
    a. Nahe
    b. Rheingau
    c. Ahr
    d. Franken

18. Pinot Noir-based rosé, known as _____, is a specialty of the _____ region.
    a. Halbtrocken, Mittelrhein
    b. Abfüller, Franken
    c. Weissherbst, Baden
    d. Gutswein, Mosel

CENTRAL AND EASTERN EUROPE

CHAPTER FOURTEEN

LEARNING OBJECTIVES

After studying this chapter, the candidate should be able to:

- Discuss the physical location and general climate of Austria's major wine regions.
- Recognize Austria's signature grape variety and other important grapes.
- Describe Austrian wine law and the hierarchy of Austrian wine designations.
- Discuss the other main wines and wine regions of central and eastern Europe.

EXERCISE 1: AUSTRIA: MAP EXERCISE

Using the map and the terms listed below, identify the regional wine designations of Austria.

Kamptal DAC
Carnuntum DAC
Wachau DAC
Neusiedlersee DAC
Weststeiermark DAC

Wagram DAC
Mittelburgenland DAC
Weinviertel DAC
Südsteiermark DAC
Vulkanland Steiermark DAC

Rosalia DAC
Traisental DAC
Thermenregion DAC
Wiener Gemischter Satz DAC

Kremstal DAC
Leithaberg DAC
Eisenberg DAC

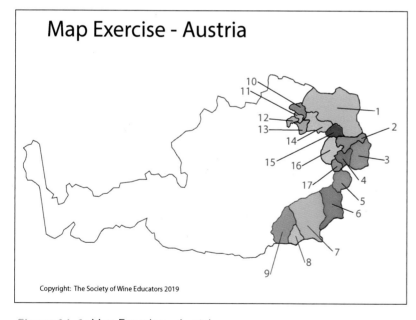

Figure 14-1: Map Exercise – Austria

1. _____

2. _____

3. _____

4. _____

5. _____

6. _____

7. _____

8. _____

9. _____

10. _____

11. _____

12. _____

13. _____

14. _____

15. _____

16. _____

17. _____

Fill in the blanks or give a short answer for the following statements or questions.

1. What percentage of Austria's wine production is white wine? _____

2. What portion of Austria's vineyards are planted with Grüner Veltliner? _____

3. What are some typical descriptors used for a young white wine made with Grüner Veltliner?

   _____

4. What grape is a cross between Riesling and Madeleine Royale?

   _____

5. In Austria, what alternative name is often used for Chardonnay? _____

6. What is the most widely planted red grape in Austria? _____

7. What red grape is also known as Lemberger or Kékfrankos?

   _____

8. What scale is used to measure must weight in Austria? _____

9. What terms may be used for an Austrian wine produced using dried grapes?

   _____

10. What is the lowest level on the Austrian Prädikat, and how does this differ from Germany's Prädikat system?

    _____

    _____

    _____

11. Austria has _____ grape varieties authorized for use in wines at the Qualitätswein and Prädikatswein level. Of these, _____ are red varieties and _____ are white.

12. Many of Austria's quality wine subregions are classified as _____ and have strict AOC-style regulations as to what type and styles of wine may be produced using the classification title.

Fill in the blanks or give a short answer for the following statements or questions.

1. _____ is the largest wine region (Weinbaugebiete) in Austria in terms of both geographical area and vineyard plantings.

2. The wines of the Weinviertel DAC are produced using 100% _____ _____ grapes.

3. The Mittelburgenland DAC produces red wines based on the _____ _____ grape variety.

4. The _____ DAC, located within the larger Leithaberg region, is approved for the production of sweet, botrytis-affected white wines.

5. The Neusiedlersee DAC produces red wines based on the _____ grape variety.

6. _____ Veltliner is a pink-skinned grape grown in the Wagram DAC.

7. Wine taverns known as _____ are popular in and around the vineyards of Vienna.

8. The DAC that surrounds the city of Vienna is known as the _____

   _____ .

9. The _____ DAC, located to the west of Lake Neusiedl, produces single-varietal white wines, blended white wines, and red wines based on the Blaufränkisch grape.

10. The _____ DAC is known for its volcanic soils.

11. The _____ DAC is known for the production of Schilcher rosé.

12. The city of Vienna lies on the _____ River.

13. What is the largest subregion of the Niederösterreich region? _____ .

14. The _____ DAC, located in a steep valley along the Danube River, is known for its loess-and gneiss-based soil.

15. The Schilcher grape variety is also known as _____ .

16. The _____ DAC—with 60% of its vineyards planted to Grüner Veltliner— is one of the smallest producers in Austria (in terms of volume).

Match each of the following terms with its appropriate definition. Each term will be used only once.

Rkatsiteli   Bulgaria   Chasselas   Rubin   Tribidrag
Kvevri   Saperavi   Slovenia   Tokaji Aszú   Graševina
Romania   Egri Bikavér   Croatia   Kékfrankos   Crimea

1. _____   The leading red grape of the country of Georgia

2. _____   Alternative name used for the Blaufränkisch grape variety

3. _____   The leading white grape variety of Switzerland

4. _____   A dessert wine produced in northern Hungary

5. _____   A Hungarian red wine traditionally known as Bull's Blood

6. _____   Half of this country's wine is produced in the Podravje region

7. _____   Country with many vineyard areas interspersed among islands and inlets formed by the Kvarner Gulf

8. _____   A grape variety known to be a Nebbiolo X Syrah cross

9. _____   An egg-shaped, earthenware vessel traditionally used in the country of Georgia

10. _____   Home of the Novy Svet Winery

11. _____   The predominant white grape variety of Eastern Europe

12. _____   The native Fetească Neagră grape is considered to be the flagship red variety of this country

13. _____   White grape variety also known as Welschriesling

14. _____   Country located to the south of (and across the Danube River from) Romania

15. _____   Grape variety also known as Crljenak Kaštelanski, Zinfandel, or Primitivo

1. Which of the following grape varieties is sometimes known as Morillon?
   a. Zinfandel
   b. Chasselas
   c. Riesling
   d. Chardonnay

2. What is the most widely planted red grape variety in Austria?
   a. Pinot Noir
   b. Zweigelt
   c. St. Laurent
   d. Merlot

3. Which of the following is a requirement of Bergwein?
   a. The grapes are grown on steeply-graded mountain slopes.
   b. The wine is produced using a field blend of at least four grape varieties.
   c. The wine is produced using partially botrytis-affected grapes.
   d. The wine is produced from grapes that are allowed to dry for 3 months after harvest.

4. A wine with the term *Federspiel* on the label is most likely from which of the following regions?
   a. Vienna
   b. Leithaberg
   c. The Wachau
   d. The Mosel

5. Which of the following is an Austrian DAC approved for both Riesling and Grüner Veltliner?
   a. Mittelrhein
   b. Kremstal
   c. Weinviertel
   d. Eisenberg

6. The _____ DAC is approved for red wines based on the Zweigelt grape variety; in 2020, it was approved for sweet white wines as well.
   a. Neusiedlersee
   b. Traisental
   c. Kamptal
   d. Leithaberg

7. Where is Egri Bikavér produced?
   a. Croatia
   b. Romania
   c. Austria
   d. Hungary

8. Which of the following countries is not a member of the European Union?
   a. Switzerland
   b. Croatia
   c. Austria
   d. Romania

9. What is the leading white grape variety of Switzerland?
   a. Rkatsiteli
   b. Tarnave
   c. Chasselas
   d. Airén

10. Which of the following grape varieties is also known as Fendant?
    a. Chardonnay
    b. Chasselas
    c. Pinot Noir
    d. Muscat

11. Which of the following is the most widely grown white grape variety in Georgia?
    a. Fetească Alba
    b. Saperavi
    c. Rkatsiteli
    d. Steinfeder

12. Which of the following is true concerning the wine industry of Croatia?
    a. Over 80% of the wine produced is red wine.
    b. The wine country is divided into three broad regions.
    c. The majority of the high-quality wine is produced in the inland region.
    d. The most widely grown grape variety is Graševina.

118

EASTERN MEDITERRANEAN

CHAPTER FIFTEEN

LEARNING OBJECTIVES

After studying this chapter, the candidate should be able to:

- Identify the physical location and general climate of Greece's major wine regions.
- Understand the hierarchy of wine designations used in Greece.

- Recognize significant appellations in Greece and their primary grape varieties.
- Describe the style and source of Commandaria.
- Understand the general status of the Israeli wine industry.

EXERCISE 1: GREECE: MAP EXERCISE

Using numbers 1 through 7 and the terms listed below, identify the major administrative regions of Greece.

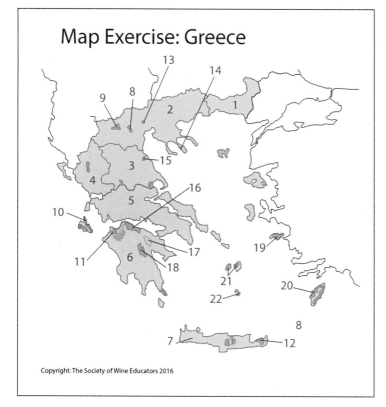

Thessalia
Crete
Central Greece
Macedonia
Thrace
Epirus
Peloponnese

1. _____

2. _____

3. _____

4. _____

5. _____

6. _____

7. _____

Figure 15-1: Map Exercise – Greece

Using numbers 8 – 22 and the terms listed below, identify the following Greek wine-producing areas.

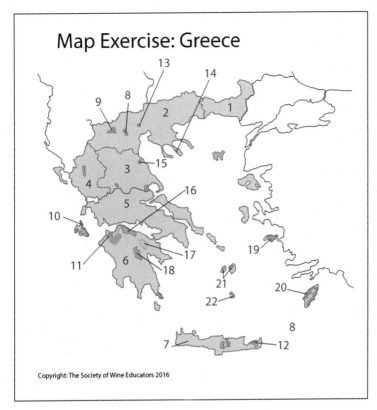

Figure 15-1: Map Exercise – Greece

Slopes of Meliton PDO
Muscat of Rio Patras PDO
Mavrodaphne of Cephalonia PDO
Mantinia PDO
Naoussa PDO
Rapsani PDO
Rhodes PDO
Malvasia Sitia PDO
Goumenissa PDO
Santorini PDO
Samos PDO
Amynteo PDO
Nemea PDO
Paros PDO
Muscat of Patras PDO

8. _____

9. _____

10. _____

11. _____

12. _____

13. _____

14. _____

15. _____

16. _____

17. _____

18. _____

19. _____

20. _____

21. _____

22. _____

Match each of the following terms with its appropriate definition. Each term will be used only once.

Onomasía Proeléfseos Anotéras Piótitos (OPAP)
Topikos Oínos (TO)
Assyrtiko
Retsina
Agiorgitiko
Onomasía Proeléfseos Eleghoméni (OPE)
Roditis
Mavrodaphne

Xinomavro
Onomasía Katá Parádosi (OKP)
Verdea
Moschofilero
Epitrapézios Oínos (EO)
Muscat
Vinsanto

1. _____ Red grape used in the production of fortified wines in Patras

2. _____ Traditional Greek wine flavored with resin

3. _____ Dessert wine specialty of Santorini

4. _____ Greek term for regional, PGI-level wine

5. _____ Designation for the certain traditional Greek wines

6. _____ Top-tier Greek wine designation; typically reserved for sweet wines

7. _____ A pink-skinned grape variety native to the Peloponnese

8. _____ Red grape of the Naoussa PDO

9. _____ Top quality designation used for dry, unfortified wines

10. _____ High-acid white wine grape variety originally from Santorini

11. _____ A traditional, oxidative white wine

12. _____ Red variety known as "Saint George's grape"

13. _____ Classification for standard Greek table wine

14. _____ White grape used in the sweet wines of Samos and Patras

15. _____ White grape used in the dry wines of the Patras PDO

Fill in the blanks or give a short answer for the following statements or questions.

1. What is the largest red wine appellation in Greece? _____

2. The Greek islands of Samos, Santorini, and Rhodes are located in the _____ Sea.

3. The Greek islands of Corfu and Cephalonia are located in the _____ Sea.

4. The _____ Peninsula has the highest concentration of vineyards in all of Greece.

5. What red grape, widely planted throughout Greece, is also known as "acid black"? _____
_____

6. What are the two main grape varieties used in the production of Commandaria? _____
_____

7. A complex, traditional aging system, known as the _____ system, is sometimes used in the aging of Commandaria.

8. Most of Lebanon's vineyards are located in the _____ area.

9. _____ is, by reputation, the leading producer of Lebanese wine.

10. The _____ Winery, originally established in the 1880s, is now the largest winery in Israel.

11. Simcha Blass is credited with inventing _____.

12. The _____ grape variety was created in 1972 as a Carignan X Sousão cross.

13. The _____ is a semi-arid, desert-like region located in southern Israel.

14. Much of Israel's quality wine is produced in _____, a high-elevation region located in the north of the country.

15. In 1855, the _____ Wine Estate (and Monastery) was established near Jerusalem.

1. Grapevines on the windy island of Santorini are often trained into the shape of a _____.
   a. Pergola
   b. Lyre
   c. Basket
   d. Telephone pole

2. Which of the following is the largest red wine appellation in Greece?
   a. Santorini
   b. Rhodes
   c. Samos
   d. Nemea

3. Which of the following areas is located farthest north?
   a. Naoussa PDO
   b. Samos PDO
   c. Patras PDO
   d. Nemea PDO

4. Which of the following is a sweet wine produced on the island of Santorini?
   a. Kava
   b. Rasteau
   c. Vinsanto
   d. Patras

5. Which of the following is a red grape variety?
   a. Moschofilero
   b. Xinomavro
   c. Assyritiko
   d. Roditis

6. The Onomasía Katá Parádosi (OKP) classification is a special subcategory designed to protect which of the following wines?
   a. Commandaria
   b. Vinsanto
   c. Retsina
   d. Kava

7. Which of the following is a pink-skinned grape, widely grown in the Peloponnese?
   a. Mavrodaphne
   b. Assyritiko
   c. Agiorgitiko
   d. Moschofilero

8. The Bekaa Valley is one of the leading wine-producing regions of which of the following countries?
   a. Lebanon
   b. Greece
   c. Israel
   d. Türkiye (Turkey)

9. Which of the following areas is located farthest south?
   a. Rapsani PDO
   b. Muscat of Rhodes PDO
   c. Slopes of Meliton PDO
   d. Muscat of Rio Patras PDO

10. Which of the following best describes Commandaria?
    a. An amber-colored dessert wine
    b. A dry white wine
    c. A sparkling red wine
    d. A red wine flavored with pine resin

124

LEARNING OBJECTIVES

After studying this chapter, the candidate should be able to:

- Identify the general role and position of the United States in the global wine industry.
- Describe the differences between native American grapes, French-American hybrids, and vinifera.
- Discuss the differences between American viticultural areas and European appellations.
- Recall the major required and optional elements of a wine label in the United States.

- Recall the minimum content requirements for the use of place-of-origin terms, vintage dates, and grape variety names on a US wine label.
- Recognize the importance of California to the US wine industry.
- Identify the primary appellations, climatic zones, and major grapes of California, Washington, Oregon, and New York.
- Discuss the major wine-producing regions of Canada and Mexico.

EXERCISE 1: US WINE HISTORY: SHORT ANSWER/FILL IN THE BLANK

Fill in the blanks or give a short answer for the following statements or questions.

1. During what years was Prohibition in effect in the United States? _____

2. What 1849 event led to an increase in the population in California and, eventually, to an increased demand for California wine? _____

3. John Patchett and Charles Krug are among the founders of the first commercial wineries in _____ County.

4. Who was the founder of Sonoma's Buena Vista Winery? _____

5. What Russian-born California winemaker was known as the *dean of American winemakers*? _____

6. Who is remembered for creating Ohio-grown, Catawba-based sparkling wines (in the 1830s)? _____

7. What British wine merchant organized the 1976 Paris Tasting? _____

8. What iconic style of American wine was first created at Sutter Home Winery (in 1972)? _____

For each of the following potential elements of a wine label, determine if it is required, optional, or not permitted according to the labeling laws of the United States.

Item	Required?	Optional?	Not Permitted?
1. Vintage date _____	☐	☐	☐
2. Health claims _____	☐	☐	☐
3. Alcohol content _____	☐	☐	☐
4. Grape variety/varieties _____	☐	☐	☐
5. "Estate Bottled" _____	☐	☐	☐
6. Label art _____	☐	☐	☐
7. Name of the bottler/importer _____	☐	☐	☐
8. Address of the bottler/importer _____	☐	☐	☐
9. Net contents (volume) _____	☐	☐	☐
10. Appellation of origin _____	☐	☐	☐
11. Sulfite statement _____	☐	☐	☐
12. Brand name _____	☐	☐	☐

Mark each of the following statements as true or false.

1. _____ Some European place-names, including Chablis, Burgundy, and Chianti, are considered by the United States to be "semi-generic."

2. _____ Semi-generic place-names may be used on a US wine label as long as an American geographic term is also used, provided that the label was approved prior to March, 2006.

3. _____ The use of the term *Champagne* has never been permitted on a US wine label.

4. _____ A standard 750 ml wine bottle contains 22 fluid ounces.

5. _____ If a single vinifera grape variety appears on a California wine label, then the wine must contain a minimum of 70% of the named variety.

6. _____ Oregon Pinot Noir must contain a minimum of 90% Pinot Noir grapes.

7. _____ In the US, varietal wines produced with native North American grape varieties (*Vitis labrusca*) must contain a minimum of 75% of the named grape variety.

8. _____ The term *Meritage* refers to wines that are made with Bordeaux grape varieties.

9. _____ If a wine's stated place of origin is a country, then a minimum of 75% of the wine in the bottle must be from the named country.

10. _____ If a wine's stated place of origin is the state of California, then a minimum of 90% of the wine in the bottle must be from California.

11. _____ In general, if a wine's appellation of origin is a specific AVA, then a minimum of 85% of the wine must be from the named AVA.

12. _____ If a wine's stated place of origin is a specific vineyard, then 100% of the wine must be from the named vineyard.

13. _____ The term *estate bottled* may not be used on American wines.

14. _____ The term *old vine* has no legal definition in the United States, but it is permitted to be used on a wine label, provided the term is not misleading.

15. _____ According to the TTB, the term *Fumé Blanc* is an approved synonym for *Sauvignon Blanc* in the United States.

Using the map and the terms listed below, identify the following AVAs of Napa County.

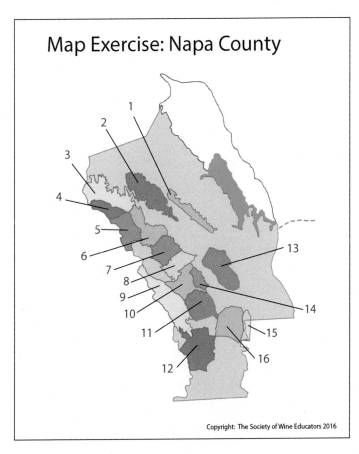

Figure 16-1: Map Exercise – Napa County

Yountville AVA
St. Helena AVA
Coombsville AVA
Oak Knoll District AVA
Wild Horse Valley AVA
Calistoga AVA
Atlas Peak AVA
Diamond Mountain
  District AVA

Spring Mountain District
  AVA
Oakville AVA
Los Carneros AVA
Chiles Valley District
  AVA
Stags Leap District AVA
Howell Mountain AVA
Rutherford AVA
Mount Veeder AVA

1. _____

2. _____

3. _____

4. _____

5. _____

6. _____

7. _____

8. _____

9. _____

10. _____

11. _____

12. _____

13. _____

14. _____

15. _____

16. _____

Using the map and the terms listed below, identify the following AVAs of Sonoma County.

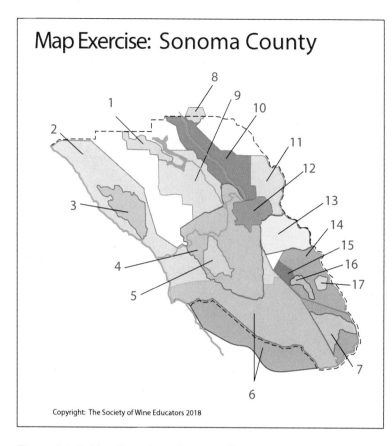

Figure 16-2: Map Exercise – Sonoma County

Sonoma Mountain AVA
Chalk Hill AVA
Green Valley AVA
Fountaingrove District AVA
Dry Creek Valley AVA
Petaluma Gap AVA
Bennett Valley AVA
Russian River Valley AVA
Pine Mountain-Cloverdale Peak AVA
Alexander Valley AVA
Sonoma Valley AVA
Sonoma Coast AVA
Fort Ross-Seaview AVA
Moon Mountain District AVA
Rockpile AVA
Los Carneros AVA
Knights Valley AVA

1. _____

2. _____

3. _____

4. _____

5. _____

6. _____

7. _____

8. _____

9. _____

10. _____

11. _____

12. _____

13. _____

14. _____

15. _____

16. _____

17. _____

Match each of the following terms with its appropriate definition. Each term will be used only once.

Pinot Noir   Bennett Valley   Los Carneros   Fort Ross-Seaview   Wild Horse Valley
Zinfandel   Chiles Valley   Howell Mountain   Rutherford   Cole Ranch
Cabernet Sauvignon Green Valley   Anderson Valley   Mendocino Ridge   Fountaingrove District
Petaluma Gap

1. _____ Leading red grape variety of Napa County

2. _____ Red wine grape particularly well-suited to the Russian River Valley AVA

3. _____ Mendocino County AVA well-known for sparkling wine

4. _____ Napa AVA often noted for its "dust"

5. _____ AVA shared between Napa and Sonoma Counties

6. _____ AVA shared between Napa and Solano Counties

7. _____ Subregion of the Russian River Valley AVA

8. _____ Subregion of the Sonoma Valley AVA

9. _____ AVA often referred to as "Islands in the Sky"

10. _____ AVA shared between Sonoma and Marin Counties

11. _____ Subregion of the Sonoma Coast AVA

12. _____ Leading red grape variety of the Dry Creek Valley AVA

13. _____ The smallest AVA in California

14. _____ The only elevation-specific AVA of Napa County

15. _____ Napa County AVA, located somewhat to the east of the valley floor, that extends into the Vaca Mountains

16. _____ AVA located (in Sonoma) just north of the Sonoma Valley AVA

Using the map and the terms listed below, identify the following AVAs of California's North Central Coast.

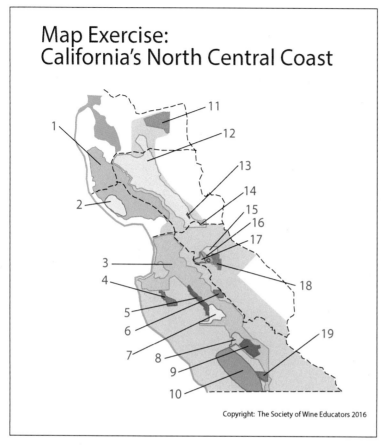

San Benito AVA
San Ysidro District AVA
San Bernabe AVA
Mount Harlan AVA
Livermore Valley AVA
Carmel Valley AVA
Chalone AVA
Hames Valley AVA
Arroyo Seco AVA
Ben Lomond Mountain AVA
San Lucas AVA
Pacheco Pass AVA
Santa Lucia Highlands AVA
Cienega Valley AVA
Paicines AVA
Santa Clara Valley AVA
Santa Cruz Mountains AVA
Monterey AVA
San Antonio Valley AVA

Figure 16-3: Map Exercise – California's North Central Coast

1. _____
2. _____
3. _____
4. _____
5. _____
6. _____
7. _____
8. _____
9. _____
10. _____

11. _____
12. _____
13. _____
14. _____
15. _____
16. _____
17. _____
18. _____
19. _____

Match each of the following terms with its appropriate definition. Each term will be used only once.

Hames Valley   Edna Valley   El Dorado   Los Olivos
Livermore Valley   Lake County   Arroyo Seco   Alisos Canyon
Paso Robles   Sta. Rita Hills   Sierra Foothills
Guenoc Valley   Alta Mesa   Central Valley
Santa Maria Valley   Monterey   Ben Lomond Mountain

1. _____ AVA found within Lake County

2. _____ County that produces nearly 20% of California's Chardonnay

3. _____ Sub-appellation located in the cooler portion of the Monterey AVA

4. _____ Sub-appellation located in the warmer portion of the Monterey AVA

5. _____ Large AVA with 11 sub-appellations, including San Juan Creek and Templeton Gap

6. _____ Cool-climate AVA located in San Luis Obispo County

7. _____ Santa Barbara AVA located on the western (and therefore cooler) side of the Santa Ynez Valley AVA

8. _____ Subregion of the Santa Cruz Mountains AVA

9. _____ Large expanse of fertile land tucked between California's Coast Range and the Sierra Nevada Mountains

10. _____ Sub-appellation of the Lodi AVA

11. _____ Sub-appellation of the Sierra Foothills AVA

12. _____ Large AVA that contains only 1% of California's wine grape acreage

13. _____ AVA located in the far north of the Central Coast AVA

14. _____ County that, according to the EPA, has the purest air quality in California

15. _____ Santa Barbara AVA located north of the Santa Ynez River and just east of the Ballard Canyon AVA

16. _____ The northernmost AVA in Santa Barbara County

17. _____ Santa Barbara County AVA known as a "Goldilocks Zone" for Rhône grapes

Using the map and the terms listed below, identify the following AVAs of Washington State.

Red Mountain AVA
Columbia Gorge AVA
Walla Walla Valley AVA
Yakima Valley AVA
Wahluke Slope AVA
Snipes Mountain AVA

Lake Chelan AVA
Columbia Valley AVA
Naches Heights AVA
Rattlesnake Hills AVA
Lewis-Clark Valley AVA
Horse Heaven Hills AVA

Puget Sound AVA
Ancient Lakes of Columbia
   Valley AVA
Royal Slope AVA
White Bluffs AVA

The Burn of Columbia
   Valley AVA
Goose Gap AVA/Candy
   Mountain AVA
Rocky Reach AVA

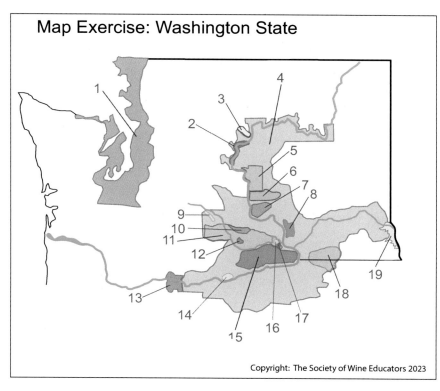

Figure 16-4: Map Exercise – Washington State

1. _____
2. _____
3. _____
4. _____
5. _____
6. _____
7. _____
8. _____
9. _____
10. _____
11. _____
12. _____
13. _____
14. _____
15. _____
16. _____
17. _____
18. _____
19. _____

Fill in the blanks or give a short answer for the following statements or questions.

1. State law requires that any wine using a Washington State appellation contain a minimum of _____ percent Washington State grapes.

2. The state of Washington is the _____ largest producer of vinifera wine in the United States.

3. The _____ of the Cascades results in near-desert conditions for much of eastern Washington State.

4. Due to the state's _____, Washington has more total sunshine hours than California.

5. The leading red grapes of Washington State are _____ and _____. While _____ is grown in smaller quantities, it often draws some of the highest critical acclaim.

6. Chardonnay is the leading white grape of Washington State, but the area is also a premier growing spot for _____, the number two grape variety.

7. The _____ AVA, one of the largest in the country, encompasses most of Washington State's vineyard area.

8. The _____ AVA was Washington State's first appellation.

9. The _____ AVA was named for a deep layer of lakebed sediment known as the Ringold Formation.

10. The _____ AVA is the only Washington State AVA located on the western side of the Cascades.

11. The _____ AVA is named for the numerous pothole lakes formed by the Missoula Floods.

12. The _____ AVA, shared with Oregon, is located where the Columbia River cuts a narrow passage through the Cascade Mountains.

13. The _____ AVA is shared between Washington State and Idaho.

14. The _____ of Columbia Valley AVA is located along the _____ bank of the Columbia River.

Using the map and the terms listed below, identify the regional wine designations of Oregon.

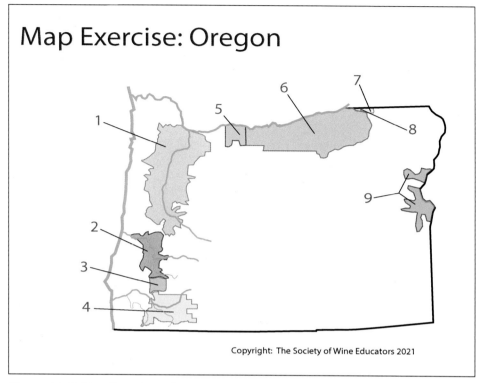

Figure 16-5: Map Exercise – Oregon

Walla Walla Valley AVA
Columbia Gorge AVA
Snake River Valley AVA
Rogue Valley AVA
Columbia Valley AVA
Umpqua Valley AVA
The Rocks of Milton-
   Freewater AVA
Willamette Valley AVA
Southern Oregon AVA

1. _____

2. _____

3. _____

4. _____

5. _____

6. _____

7. _____

8. _____

9. _____

Fill in the blanks or give a short answer for the following statements or questions.

1. What three UC Davis graduates are often credited with being the "pioneers" of the modern Oregon wine industry?

    _____

2. For what three types of wine has Oregon gained particularly wide acclaim?

    _____

3. What top Burgundy producer established a wine estate in Oregon in 1988, and what is the name of the winery?

    _____

    _____

4. What three AVAs straddle the Oregon-Washington State border?

    _____

    _____

5. The Willamette Valley AVA, located about _____ from the Pacific Ocean, is home to nearly _____ of Oregon's vineyards.

6. The tiny _____ AVA is located in the Oregon side of the larger Walla Walla Valley AVA, which is itself shared with _____ _____.

7. The _____ AVA combines the Rogue Valley and Umpqua Valley AVAs.

8. The Rogue Valley AVA has one sub-appellation, the _____ AVA.

9. What are the two sub-appellations of the Umpqua Valley AVA? _____

    _____

Using the map and the terms listed below, identify the AVAs of the Willamette Valley.

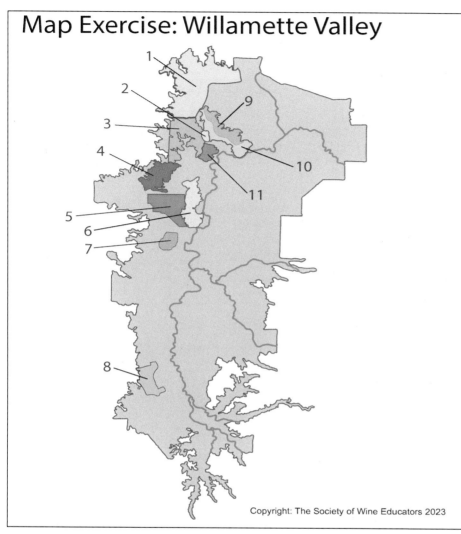

Eola-Amity Hills AVA
Ribbon Ridge AVA
McMinnville AVA
Dundee Hills AVA
Chehalem Mountains AVA
Yamhill-Carlton AVA
Mount Pisgah-Polk County AVA
Van Duzer Corridor AVA
Laurelwood District AVA
Tualatin Hills AVA
Lower Long Tom AVA

Figure 16-6: Map Exercise – Willamette Valley

1. _____

2. _____

3. _____

4. _____

5. _____

6. _____

7. _____

8. _____

9. _____

10. _____

11. _____

Fill in the blanks or give a short answer for the following statements or questions.

1. New York's _____ AVA and its two sub-AVAs, the _____ AVA and the _____ AVA, account for over 85% of the state's wine production.

2. A viticulturist from Russia named _____ is credited with championing the planting of vinifera grapes in the cold-climate environment of New York State.

3. With a climate similar to Germany's, New York State does well with grapes from the _____ _____ species and cold-hardy _____, in addition to vinifera varieties such as Riesling and Cabernet Franc.

4. The _____ AVA is located two hours east of New York City. It has two sub-appellations, including the North Fork of Long Island AVA and the _____ AVA.

5. The Brotherhood Winery is located in the _____ AVA, located north of New York City.

6. Appellations (geographical indications) in British Columbia and Ontario are known as

   _____ .

7. The leading appellation of Ontario—home to as much as 85% of the province's vines—is

   _____ .

8. In the 1970s, the _____ Winery (in Ontario) led the way in building international recognition for a Canadian dessert wine known as _____ .

9. A long, narrow valley known as the _____ is the leading region for wine production in British Columbia.

10. The province of Nova Scotia is famous for its signature white wine blend, known as

    _____ .

11. The main wine region in Baja California is the _____ , located near the city of _____ .

12. _____ , located in the Mexican state of Coahuila, is one of the oldest wineries in North America.

1. What is the largest Icewine-producing region in the world?
   a. Washington State
   b. Ontario
   c. British Columbia
   d. New York's Finger Lakes

2. Which of the following elements are *all* required on a US wine label?
   a. Alcohol content, address of the bottler, and vintage date
   b. Brand name, net contents by volume, and appellation of origin
   c. Name of the bottler, grape varieties, and brand name
   d. Brand name, alcohol content, and net contents by volume

3. Which of the following wines could be labeled with the term *Meritage*?
   a. A red blend of Cabernet Sauvignon, Cabernet Franc, and Merlot
   b. A red blend of Petit Verdot, Malbec, and Pinot Noir
   c. A white blend of Sauvignon Blanc and Chenin Blanc
   d. A white blend of Chardonnay and Semillon

4. If a wine's appellation of origin is Napa Valley, what percentage of its contents must be from the Napa Valley AVA?
   a. 100%
   b. Minimum of 95%
   c. Minimum of 85%
   d. Minimum of 75%

5. If a wine is labeled as "Napa Valley Sauvignon Blanc," what percentage of the wine must be Sauvignon Blanc?
   a. 100%
   b. Minimum of 95%
   c. Minimum of 85%
   d. Minimum of 75%

6. What is the leading red grape of Napa County?
   a. Merlot
   b. Cabernet Sauvignon
   c. Pinot Noir
   d. Zinfandel

7. Which of the following areas is NOT a sub-appellation of the Willamette Valley AVA?
   a. Van Duzer Corridor
   b. Eola-Amity Hills
   c. Dundee Hills
   d. Rocky Reach

8. Which of the following AVAs is a subregion of the Russian River Valley AVA?
   a. Fort Ross-Seaview
   b. Green Valley
   c. Chiles Valley
   d. Los Carneros

9. Of the following AVAs, which is best known for Zinfandel?
   a. Dry Creek Valley
   b. McMinnville
   c. Anderson Valley
   d. Dundee Hills

10. Of the following AVAs, which is best known for Pinot Noir?
    a. Knights Valley
    b. Borden Ranch
    c. Eola-Amity Hills
    d. Paso Robles

11. Which of the following is a Mendocino County AVA well-known for sparkling wine?
    a. Rockpile
    b. Anderson Valley
    c. Ribbon Ridge
    d. Red Mountain

12. Which of the following appellations is particularly well-known for Washington State Syrah?
    a. McMinnville
    b. Arroyo Grande
    c. Edna Valley
    d. Royal Slope

13. Which of the following AVAs covers a large expanse of land, yet contains only 1% of California's vineyard acreage?
    a. Livermore Valley
    b. Central Valley
    c. Lodi
    d. Sierra Foothills

14. The Paso Robles AVA is located within which of the following counties?
    a. El Dorado
    b. Monterey
    c. San Luis Obispo
    d. Santa Barbara

15. Which of the following are *all* subregions of the Lodi AVA?
    a. Jahant, Borden Ranch, and Alta Mesa
    b. Alta Mesa, Hames Valley, and Borden Ranch
    c. Edna Valley, Clements Hills, and Sloughhouse
    d. Borden Ranch, Snipes Mountain, and Ribbon Ridge

16. Which of the following mountain ranges provides a rain shadow for much of eastern Washington State?
    a. The Coastal Range
    b. The Cascades
    c. The Caribou Mountains
    d. The Snake River Range

17. David Lett and Dick Erath are considered two of the "pioneers" of the wine industry in which of the following areas?
    a. Napa Valley
    b. Finger Lakes
    c. Mendocino
    d. Oregon

18. Which of the following wine regions is most affected by the Niagara Escarpment?
    a. Okanagan Valley
    b. Ontario
    c. Hudson River Region
    d. Clear Lake

19. Due to the region's climate, which of the following grapes are considered to be best suited for the Finger Lakes AVA?
    a. Zinfandel and Sauvignon Blanc
    b. Syrah and Riesling
    c. Cabernet Franc and Riesling
    d. Chardonnay and Malbec

20. During what years was Prohibition in effect in the United States?
    a. 1917–1925
    b. 1920–1933
    c. 1915–1929
    d. 1925–1933

SOUTH AMERICA

CHAPTER SEVENTEEN

LEARNING OBJECTIVES

After studying this chapter, the candidate should be able to:

- Recognize the importance of latitude and elevation for grape growing in South America.
- Describe the influences of the Andes on grape growing in Argentina and Chile.
- Discuss the major wine regions of Argentina and Chile.
- Recall the significant grape varieties grown in Argentina and Chile.
- Understand the general status of the wine industry in Brazil and Uruguay.

EXERCISE 1: ARGENTINA: SHORT ANSWER/FILL IN THE BLANK

Fill in the blanks or give a short answer for the following statements or questions.

1. What climatic and geographical features combine to make the western foothills of Argentina an excellent area for wine grapes?

   _____

2. The high-altitude vineyards of Argentina are often shaken by the fierce, sometimes damaging _____ winds.

3. What weather threat can affect the vineyards of Argentina at harvest time?

   _____

4. What is the leading red grape of Argentina?_____

5. Argentina's key white grape, _____, has recently been determined to be three distinct varieties.

6. Argentina currently has two areas— Luján de Cuyo and San Rafael—that qualify for _____ _____ status.

7. Argentina grows a large quantity of grapes from the _____ family; however, these have traditionally been primarily used for bulk-style and other inexpensive wine.

Using the map and the terms listed below, identify the following wine regions of Argentina.

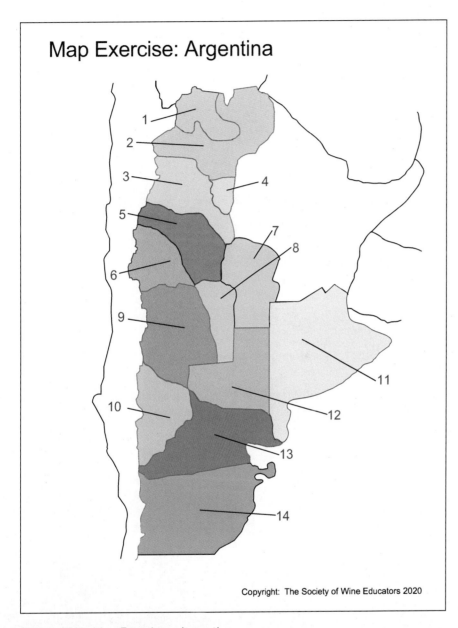

Figure 17-1: Map Exercise – Argentina

Chubut
Córdoba
Buenos Aires
Tucamán
Mendoza
Salta
Río Negro
Catamarca
San Juan
La Rioja
Jujuy
Neuquén
La Pampa
San Luis

1. _____

2. _____

3. _____

4. _____

5. _____

6. _____

7. _____

8. _____

9. _____

10. _____

11. _____

12. _____

13. _____

14. _____

Match each of the following terms with its appropriate definition. Each term will be used only once.

Salta	Reserva	Neuquén	Chubut
Pedro Giménez	San Juan	La Rioja	Jujuy
Río Negro	Cafayate	Bonarda Argentina	San Rafael
Vinos finos	Mendoza	Luján de Cuyo	Córdoba

1. _____ Province with close to 17% of Argentina's vineyards, making it the second-largest grape-producing province in the country

2. _____ Province particularly well-known for high-altitude Torrontés Riojano

3. _____ Province that contains the Famatina mountain range

4. _____ Province that contains close to 75% of Argentina's vineyards

5. _____ Term used to designate the best wines of Argentina

6. _____ Home province of the ultra-high-elevation Moya Vineyard

7. _____ Label term based on minimum aging periods

8. _____ DOC region located in Mendoza's Primera Zona

9. _____ Province that contains some of the lowest elevation vineyards in Argentina

10. _____ A subregion of Salta with very high-altitude vineyards

11. _____ Province located in the geographic center of Argentina (to the east of La Rioja)

12. _____ Province located just south of Mendoza

13. _____ Red grape also known as Douce Noire

14. _____ White grape grown primarily for use in fortified wines and bulk wines

15. _____ DOC region located in South Mendoza

16. _____ Home province to a vineyard area known as Sarmiento, located near the 45th parallel (South)

Fill in the blanks or give a short answer for the following statements or questions.

1. Chile is a long, narrow country, almost _____ miles in length, and rarely more than _____ miles wide.

2. The _____, one of the driest places on earth, is located in the north of Chile, while the south contains the frozen archipelago of

_____ .

3. In part due to its natural barriers and strict quarantine policies, Chile has managed to remain free of the vineyard pest _____ .

4. Chile has a cold ocean current, known as the _____ Current, flowing along its shores from the polar seas.

5. _____ is the most widely planted grape in Chile.

6. In the 1990s, it was discovered that many of the Chilean grapes thought to be Merlot were actually _____, which is now considered by many to be the "signature" grape of Chile.

7. Some of the Chilean grapes originally thought to be Sauvignon Blanc are actually _____, and many of these vines have been replaced. However, the two grapes are not always differentiated, and both of the grapes (and their wines) are sometimes simply referred to as _____.

8. Chile has a set of geographic place-of-origin laws known as the _____ system.

9. Under Chilean law, the minimum requirement for place of origin, vintage, and variety on a wine label is _____ percent; however, many export-oriented wineries use the EU standard of _____.

10. As of 2011, three terms based on Chile's east–west geography were approved for use on Chilean wine labels. What are they?

_____

_____

_____

Using the map and the terms listed below, identify the following wine regions of Chile.

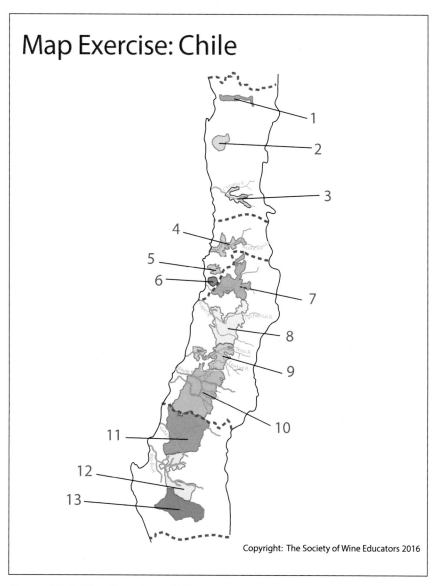

Map Exercise: Chile

Copyright: The Society of Wine Educators 2016

Figure 17-2: Map Exercise – Chile

Curicó Valley
Rapel Valley
San Antonio Valley
Itata Valley
Limarí Valley
Maipo Valley
Malleco Valley
Elqui Valley
Maule Valley
Aconcagua Valley
Bío-Bío Valley
Choapa Valley
Casablanca Valley

1. _____

2. _____

3. _____

4. _____

5. _____

6. _____

7. _____

8. _____

9. _____

10. _____

11. _____

12. _____

13. _____

Match each of the following terms with its appropriate definition. Each term will be used only once.

Bío-Bío Valley   Casablanca Valley   Leyda Valley   Austral Region
Rapel Valley   Curicó Valley   Central Valley   Elqui Valley
Choapa Valley   Maule Valley   Limarí Valley
Atacama Region   Maipo Valley   Aconcagua Valley

1. _____   Region surrounding the Chilean city of Santiago

2. _____   A cool-climate subregion of the Coquimbo, well-known for mineral-driven white wines

3. _____   The region that contains the Cachapoal and Colchagua Valleys

4. _____   The warmest subregion of Aconcagua

5. _____   A region of the Central Valley located inland, with no maritime influence

6. _____   A large area that encompasses more than 80% of Chile's vineyards

7. _____   Northern region better known for Pisco than for fine wine

8. _____   Area known for old vine Carignan and the VIGNO organization

9. _____   The southernmost extreme of winegrowing in Chile

10. _____   Area of the Southern Regions (Del Sur) increasingly planted with Riesling, Chardonnay, and Pinot Noir

11. _____   Subregion of the Aconcagua located very close to the coast and well-known for white wines

12. _____   A subzone of the San Antonio Valley known for granite soils and breezy conditions

13. _____   Area of Coquimbo, increasingly known for the country's best Syrah

14. _____   Wine area located at the narrowest point of the country

Match each of the following terms with its appropriate definition. Terms may be used more than once.

Maldonado Region	Canelones District	Altos de Pinto Bandeira DO
Serra Gaúcha	Tannat	Campanha Gaúcha
Vale do São Francisco	Graševina	Santa Catarina
Rio Grande do Sul	Montevideo	Vale dos Vinhedos DO

1. _____   Brazilian area also known as the *gaucho highlands*

2. _____   Brazilian appellation approved for traditional method sparkling wines only

3. _____   The capital city of Uruguay

4. _____   Leading grape variety of Uruguay

5. _____   Wine region located in Bahia and Pernambugo

6. _____   Grape variety also known as Harriague

7. _____   Largest-producing wine region of Brazil (in terms of volume)

8. _____   Second largest-producing wine region of Brazil (in terms of volume)

9. _____   Wine region containing close to 60% of the commercial vineyards of Uruguay

10. _____   Wine region located near the famous seaside resort town of Punta del Este

11. _____   Area known to contain some of the oldest vines in Brazil

12. _____   Brazilian state known for *vinhos de altitude*

13. _____   Brazilian area promoted to DO status in 2012

14. _____   Grape variety also known as Riesling Italico

15. _____   Brazil's leading state for commercial viticulture

1. Of the three distinct varieties of Argentine Torrontés, which is the most widely grown?
   a. Torrontés Superior
   b. Torrontés Sanjuanino
   c. Torrontés Riojano
   d. Torrontés Mendocino

2. What is the Zonda?
   a. A cold ocean current that runs up the coast of Argentina
   b. A cold ocean current that runs up the coast of Chile
   c. A hot, dry breeze that affects the Central Valley of Chile
   d. A fierce wind that may affect the vineyards of Argentina

3. What is the Humboldt Current?
   a. A cold ocean current that runs up the coast of Argentina
   b. A cold ocean current that runs up the coast of Chile
   c. A warm ocean current that runs down the coast of Chile
   d. A warm summer current that affects all of the Southern Hemisphere

4. What adverse weather condition often affects the vineyards of Argentina at harvest time?
   a. Sudden freezes
   b. Extreme humidity that can cause fungal problems
   c. Hurricanes
   d. Hailstorms

5. Which of the following grapes, once widely grown in Bordeaux, has become a "signature" grape of Chile?
   a. Malbec
   b. Petite Verdot
   c. Carmenère
   d. Semillon

6. Which of the following wine regions is located nearest to the border between Argentina and Bolivia?
   a. Jujuy
   b. Mendoza
   c. La Rioja
   d. Catamarca

7. Which of the following wine regions is known for high-altitude Torrontés?
   a. Cafayate
   b. Maule Valley
   c. Malleco Valley
   d. Río Negro

8. What is the most widely planted grape in Chile?
   a. Pinot Noir
   b. Merlot
   c. Cabernet Sauvignon
   d. Carmenère

9. Which of the following grape varieties is often mistaken for Sauvignon Blanc in Chile?
   a. Sauvignon Gris
   b. Sauvignon Vert
   c. Chenin Blanc
   d. Viognier

10. Which of the following wine regions is located closest to the city of Santiago?
    a. Mendoza
    b. Coquimbo
    c. Maipo Valley
    d. Maipú Valley

11. What was the first area to be awarded DO status in Brazil?
    a. Serra Gaúcha
    b. Serra do Sudeste
    c. Planalto Catarinense
    d. Vale dos Vinhedos

AUSTRALIA AND NEW ZEALAND

CHAPTER EIGHTEEN

LEARNING OBJECTIVES

After studying this chapter, the candidate should be able to:
- Discuss the general roles and positions of Australia and New Zealand in the global wine industry.
- Describe the basic elements of the Australian appellation system and wine labeling laws.
- Identify the physical locations and general climates of Australia's and New Zealand's major wine regions.
- Recall the significant grape varieties grown in Australia and New Zealand.

EXERCISE 1: AUSTRALIAN WINE: FILL IN THE BLANK/SHORT ANSWER

Fill in the blanks or give a short answer for the following statements or questions.

1. What is the most widely planted grape in Australia?_____

2. What three grape varieties are used in the production of Australian Rhône-style blends, known as "GSM"?

    _____

3. What is the name of Australia's place-of-origin system for wine?

    _____

4. Put the following terms used for Australian wine regions in the proper order, from largest to smallest in terms of geographic size: zone, region, state.

    _____

5. If an Australian wine uses a varietal name, what percentage of the wine must be made using the named grape variety?_____

6. Australia is the first country to require a_____ date on some styles of wine, but it is usually only seen on_____ products.

7. What nickname is often used for Australian sweet wines?_____

8. What agency is in charge of enforcing the place-of-origin system of wine in Australia?

    _____

Using the map and the terms listed below, identify the following wine regions of Australia.

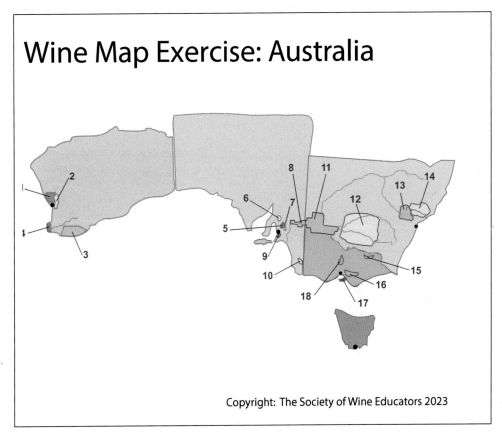

Copyright: The Society of Wine Educators 2023

Figure 18-1: Map Exercise – Australia

Heathcote	Clare Valley
Barossa Valley	Perth Hills
Mudgee	Riverina
Murray Darling	McLaren Vale
Margaret River	Yarra Valley
Hunter	Eden Valley
Rutherglen	Great Southern
Mornington Peninsula	Riverland
Swan District	
Coonawarra	

1. _____

2. _____

3. _____

4. _____

5. _____

6. _____

7. _____

8. _____

9. _____

10. _____

11. _____

12. _____

13. _____

14. _____

15. _____

16. _____

17. _____

18. _____

Match each of the following terms with its appropriate definition. Each term will be used only once.

Coonawarra   Mudgee   Mornington Peninsula   South Burnett
Barossa Valley   Hunter Valley   Perth Hills   McLaren Vale
Riverina   Rutherglen   Western Australia
Clare Valley   Margaret River   New South Wales
Yarra Valley   Murray Darling   Eden Valley

1. _____ Western Australia's premier region for Chardonnay and Sauvignon Blanc-Semillon blends

2. _____ Home to Wyndham Estate, founded in 1827

3. _____ Region located to the east of the Barossa Valley and well known for dry Riesling

4. _____ Noted for *terra rossa* soils and quality Cabernet Sauvignon

5. _____ Situated between the Gulf of Saint Vincent and the Mount Lofty Ranges

6. _____ Located just north of Sydney and known for varietal Semillon

7. _____ Named for an Aboriginal term meaning *nest in the hills*

8. _____ Home to Yering Station

9. _____ Located 80 miles/130 miles north of Adelaide; home to high-elevation vineyards planted mainly to Shiraz and Riesling

10. _____ Located in the dry interior of South Australia; home to some of the oldest vines in Australia

11. _____ Considered Australia's leading region for fortified wines

12. _____ Cool-climate region in Victoria; adjacent to Port Philip Bay

13. _____ Large region located on the border between Victoria and New South Wales

14. _____ Australian state surrounding the city of Perth

15. _____ Region located just inland of the Darling Scarp

16. _____ Large region in New South Wales; provides grape for Yellow Tail and other branded wines

17. _____ Australia's northern-most geographical indication (wine region)

Fill in the blanks or give a short answer for the following statements or questions.

1. When did New Zealand begin to establish its modern wine industry? _____

   _____

2. Where is New Zealand located? _____

   _____

3. What mountain chain runs the length of New Zealand's South Island?

   _____

4. What effect does this mountain range have on the climate of New Zealand?

   _____

   _____

5. What factors account for New Zealand's cool climate? _____

   _____

6. Due to the country's unique climate, where are most of the vineyards in New Zealand located?

   _____

   _____

7. What percentage of New Zealand's wine production is white wine? _____

8. What is the most widely planted white grape of New Zealand? _____

9. What are the other leading white wine grapes of New Zealand? _____

   _____

10. What is the most widely planted red grape of New Zealand?

   _____

11. What are the other leading red grapes of New Zealand? _____

   _____

Using the map and the terms listed below, identify the following wine regions of New Zealand.

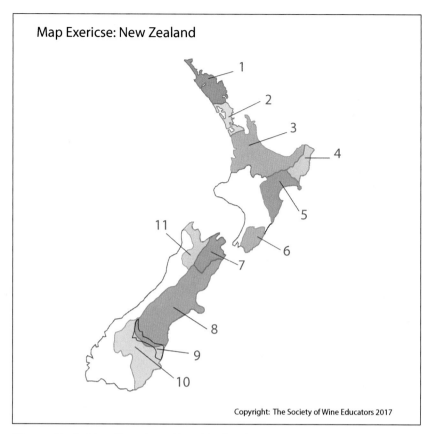

Map Exericse: New Zealand

Copyright: The Society of Wine Educators 2017

Figure 18-2: Map Exercise – New Zealand

Hawke's Bay
Marlborough
Nelson
Waikato/Bay of Plenty
Auckland
Wairarapa
Canterbury
Northland
Otago/Central Otago
Gisborne
Waitaki Valley

1. _____

2. _____

3. _____

4. _____

5. _____

6. _____

7. _____

8. _____

9. _____

10. _____

11. _____

Match each of the following terms with its appropriate definition. Each term will be used only once.

Gimblett Gravels   Canterbury   Aotearoa   Alexandra   Waikato
Marlborough   Nelson   Awatere Valley   Hawke's Bay   Waitaki Valley
Gisborne   Bannockburn   Waipara Valley   Wairau Valley   Poverty Bay

1. _____   Area located within the Gisborne region

2. _____   The self-proclaimed "Chardonnay capital of New Zealand"

3. _____   Nickname meaning "Land of the Long White Cloud"

4. _____   Region where Cloudy Bay Vineyards is located

5. _____   Area in Marlborough known for stony, alluvial soils and a cool climate (becoming drier as one heads inland)

6. _____   The most southerly sub-region of Central Otago

7. _____   Area within the Hawke's Bay region known for greywacke soils

8. _____   The only wine region on New Zealand's South Island located west of the Southern Alps

9. _____   Subregion of Marlborough located to the south of the Wairau Valley

10. _____ Another name used for the Bay of Plenty

11. _____ Large wine region that contains the city of Christchurch

12. _____ Subregion of North Canterbury

13. _____ Leading region for New Zealand Cabernet Sauvignon, Merlot, and Syrah

14. _____ Wine region located along the border of Canterbury and Otago

15. _____ Sub-region of Central Otago that often sees harvest a month before the rest of the region

1. What is Topaque?
   a. A fortified wine produced from Brown Muscat
   b. A historic wine estate, located in Victoria
   c. A fortified wine made from Muscadelle
   d. A type of Shiraz-based sparkling wine

2. Which of the following has the most impact on the climate of New Zealand?
   a. The Humboldt Current
   b. The Southern Alps
   c. The Great Dividing Range
   d. The Zonda Winds

3. Which of the following properly states the categories used in Australia's Geographical Indications, from largest in size to smallest?
   a. State, Region, Zone
   b. Region, Zone, State
   c. Zone, Region, State
   d. State, Zone, Region

4. Which of the following wine regions is located farthest south?
   a. Tasmania
   b. Canterbury
   c. Nelson
   d. Central Otago

5. If an Australian wine uses a varietal name, what percentage of the wine must be made from the named grape variety?
   a. A minimum of 75%
   b. A minimum of 80%
   c. A minimum of 85%
   d. A minimum of 95%

6. Of the following, which New Zealand wine region is most heavily planted to red grapes such as Merlot, Syrah, and Cabernet Sauvignon?
   a. Hawke's Bay
   b. Central Otago
   c. Nelson
   d. Marlborough

7. Which of the following Australian regions are both well-known for Riesling?
   a. Clare Valley and Eden Valley
   b. Margaret River and Edna Valley
   c. Hunter Valley and Clare Valley
   d. Eden Valley and McDowell Valley

8. Which of the following New Zealand wine regions is located west of the Southern Alps?
   a. Heathcote
   b. Nelson
   c. Awatere Valley
   d. Hawke's Bay

9. Which of the following Australian regions is noted for Semillon?
   a. Hunter Valley
   b. Rutherglen
   c. Tasmania
   d. Riverland

10. What is the most widely planted red grape variety in New Zealand?
    a. Merlot
    b. Gamay
    c. Pinot Noir
    d. Cabernet Sauvignon

11. Of the following, which region is located in Queensland?
    a. Mornington Peninsula
    b. Riverland
    c. Mudgee
    d. Granite Belt

12. What is the most widely planted white grape in Australia?
    a. Sauvignon Blanc
    b. Chardonnay
    c. Chenin Blanc
    d. Semillon

UNIT THREE WINE LABELS, LAWS, AND REGIONS

AFRICA

LEARNING OBJECTIVES

After studying this chapter, the candidate should be able to:

- Discuss the physical location and general climate of South Africa's major wine regions.
- Describe the significant grape varieties grown in South Africa.

- Recall South African synonyms for international grape varieties.
- Describe the basic elements of the South African appellation system and wine labeling laws.

EXERCISE 1: AFRICA: FILL IN THE BLANK/SHORT ANSWER

Fill in the blanks or give a short answer for the following statements or questions.

1. European grape vines were first planted in South Africa in the year _____, with the first wines produced in _____.

2. How does the Benguela Current influence the climate of the vineyards of South Africa?

   _____

3. What is the most widely planted grape in South Africa, and by what local name is it known?

   _____

4. What is a "Noble Late Harvest" wine? _____

5. What is a Cape Blend? _____

   _____

6. What is the name of the appellation system used in South Africa? _____

7. Put the following terms used for South African wine regions in the proper order, from largest to smallest (according to geographic size): district, geographical unit, ward, region. _____

   _____

Using the map and the terms listed below, identify the following wine regions of South Africa.

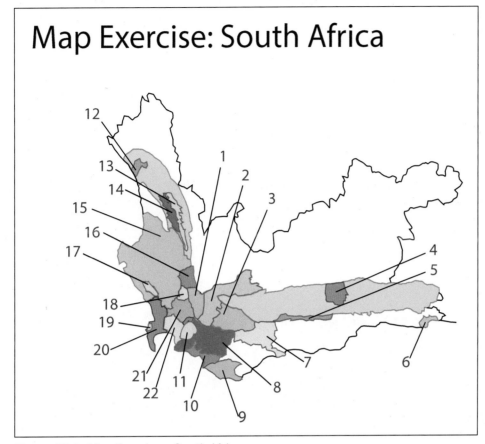

Figure 19-1: Map Exercise – South Africa

Cape Agulhas
Robertson
Constantia
Wellington
Stellenbosch
Citrusdal Valley
Elgin
Calitzdorp
Darling
Plettenberg Bay
Walker Bay
Lutzville Valley

Breedekloof
Citrusdal Mountain
Tulbagh
Worcester
Langeberg-Garcia
Overberg
Swartland
Swellendam
Paarl
Cape Town

1. _____

2. _____

3. _____

4. _____

5. _____

6. _____

7. _____

8. _____

9. _____

10. _____

11. _____

12. _____

13. _____

14. _____

15. _____

16. _____

17. _____

18. _____

19. _____

20. _____

21. _____

22. _____

Match each of the following terms with its appropriate definition. Each term will be used only once.

Devon Valley	Cape Town	Stellenbosch	Robertson	Swartland
Drakenstein Valley	Paarl	Worcester	Constantia	Algeria
Northern Cape	Franschhoek Valley	Walker Bay	Western Cape	

1. _____ Cool-climate district near the town of Hermanus; known for Chardonnay and Pinot Noir

2. _____ District known as "the Valley of Vines and Roses"

3. _____ Former French colony that once produced over 200 million cases of wine a year

4. _____ Rugged area where dry farming and untrellised vines are used

5. _____ District that contains eight wards, including Bottelary

6. _____ A ward of the Stellenbosch District

7. _____ Inland district that grows 25% of South Africa's wine (as well as table grapes and grapes for brandy)

8. _____ District in the Coastal Region whose name means "French Corner"

9. _____ Geographical Unit located well inland that contains less than 5% of the country's vines

10. _____ Ward near the city of Cape Town that is famous for a traditional desert wine

11. _____ District north of Stellenbosch that is home to many of the more familiar South African wine brands

12. _____ This Geographical Unit contains nearly 95% of South Africa's vineyards

13. _____ Area settled by French Huguenots in the 1700s

14. _____ District that contains the Constantia Ward and the Hout Bay Ward

1. In the context of South Africa's "Wine of Origin" scheme, which of the following terms represents the smallest possible geographic area?
   a. Geographical Unit
   b. Ward
   c. Region
   d. District

2. Which of the following two grapes were crossed to create the Pinotage grape variety?
   a. Pinot Noir and Merlot
   b. Cabernet Sauvignon and Pinot Noir
   c. Cinsault and Pinot Noir
   d. Shiraz and Cabernet Sauvignon

3. Which of the following climatic conditions is due to the influence of the Benguela Current?
   a. The rain shadow of the Drakenstein Mountains
   b. The "Roaring 40s" winds
   c. The Santa Ana winds
   d. The Cape Doctor

4. What is Steen?
   a. An alternative name for the Muscat of Alexandria grape variety
   b. A hybrid grape made by a Riesling X Muscat cross
   c. A botrytis-affected dessert wine
   d. An alternative name for the Chenin Blanc grape variety

5. Which of the following is a cool-climate South African wine district, well-known for Pinot Noir?
   a. Walker Bay
   b. Robertson
   c. Stellenbosch
   d. Paarl

6. Which of the following wards has a long history of producing a well-known dessert wine?
   a. Stellenbosch
   b. Breede River Valley
   c. Swartland
   d. Constantia

7. Winemaking in Franschhoek Valley was highly influenced by which group of people?
   a. Dutch traders
   b. English immigrants
   c. American settlers
   d. French Huguenots

8. The majority of South Africa's vineyard area is located within which of the following Geographical Units?
   a. The Northern Cape
   b. Breede River Valley
   c. The Western Cape
   d. Boberg

9. Which area is located farthest south?
   a. Lutzville Valley
   b. Cape Agulhas
   c. Wellington
   d. Swartland

10. The Robertson and Worcester Districts, known for table grapes, brandy and—increasingly—fine wine production are located within the _____ Region.
    a. Breede River Valley
    b. Olifants River
    c. Cape South Coast
    d. Klein Karoo

ASIA

CHAPTER TWENTY

LEARNING OBJECTIVES

After studying this chapter, the candidate should be able to:
- Describe the recent growth of the culture and business of wine in China.
- Discuss the physical location and general attributes of the wine-producing regions of China.

- Recall the main grape varieties used in Chinese wine.
- Describe the grape-based wine industry in Japan.
- Discuss the wines produced in south, Southeast, and Equatorial Asia.

EXERCISE 1: WINES OF CHINA: FILL IN THE BLANK

Fill in the blanks or give a short answer for the following statements or questions.

1. The modern era of Chinese wine production is considered to have begun in the year _____, when a _____ Dynasty diplomat imported over 100 European grape varieties into China.

2. The first modern Chinese winery, now known as the Changyu Pioneer Wine Company, Inc. is located in the _____ province.

3. By geographic area, China is the _____ largest country in the world.

4. Of the many crosses and hybrid grapes created in grape-breeding programs, _____, a Muscat Hamburg X Alicante Bouschet cross used for its deep red color, is one of the most successful.

5. The _____ grape, a Muscat Hamburg X *Vitis amurensis* hybrid, is widely used for its extreme cold resistance.

6. _____ is the name used in some parts of China to refer to the Carmenère grape variety.

7. _____, a French Cabernet Sauvignon X Grenache cross, is among the most successful red grapes in China.

8. Longyan is an aromatic grape that often goes by the name of _____.

9. Approved in 2012, _____ is the first legally regulated and geographically defined wine region in China.

Using the map and the terms listed below, identify the wine growing regions of China.

Beijing   Shanxi   Yunnan   Hebei   Xinjiang
Tianjin   Gansu   Ningxia   Shandong   Shaanxi

1. _____

2. _____

3. _____

4. _____

5. _____

6. _____

7. _____

8. _____

9. _____

10. _____

Figure 20-1: Map Exercise – China

Match each of the following terms with its appropriate definition. Terms may be used more than once.

Yunnan   Hebei   Ningxia   Shandong   Hebei   Shanxi   Xinjiang

1. _____ Home to the Sino-French Demonstration Vineyard

2. _____ Region located in the extreme west of China, neighboring the country of Kazakhstan

3. _____ Area where a French missionary first planted a French grape known as Rose Honey

4. _____ Located on the eastern edge of the Gobi Desert, this region is basically an alluvial plain of the Yellow River

5. _____ Wine region located in the area surrounding the municipality of Beijing

6. _____ The southernmost wine region in China

7. _____ The Heshuo/Hoxud wine region, which obtained Geographical Indication status in 2015, is located here

8. _____ Region located on the ocean, mostly south of the Yellow River

9. _____ The home of Grace Vineyards

10. _____ This area is home to the China Great Wall Wine Company

11. _____ Area that includes the Eastern Foot of Helan Mountain wine region

12. _____ Home to the Shangri-La Winery Company Limited

13. _____ The wines of this area were described by the famous explorer Marco Polo

Mark each of the following statements as true or false.

1. _____ Portuguese wine was first imported into Japan in the sixteenth century.

2. _____ Japanese per capita wine consumption is among the lowest in Asia.

3. _____ Japan has traditionally been more closely associated with the production and consumption of rice wine (sake) than grape-based wine.

4. _____ Four islands—Hokkaido, Honshu, Shikoku, and Kyushu—are home to a large percentage of the Japanese population.

5. _____ The Koshu grape variety, a descendant of European grapes, is considered to be native to Japan.

6. _____ Koshu is a red grape variety used mainly to produce low-tannin, fruity, semi-sweet red wines.

7. _____ According to legend, a Buddhist monk planted the first vineyards in Japan after a vision of the Yakushi Buddha.

8. _____ Muscat Bailey-A is a red hybrid grape created at the Iwanohara Winery.

9. _____ Hokkaido is considered the "main island" of Japan.

10. _____ The first modern Japanese wine was produced in 1874 at Kōfu.

11. _____ Four (out of five) of Japan's geographical indications for wine are located on the island of Hokkaido.

12. _____ In Kyushu, vines are often trained on overhead trellises known as *tanazukuri*.

13. _____ The Osaka GI specializes in the (hybrid) Delaware grape variety.

14. _____ In the 17th and 18th centuries, Japan's Sakoku Policy encouraged internationalism and allowed many freedoms in terms of commerce and trade.

15. _____ Muscat Bailey-A is sometimes used in red wine blends along with vinifera grape varieties.

1. Which of the following was considered to be modern China's first winery?
   a. Grace Vineyards
   b. Sula Winery
   c. Takla Makan Winery
   d. Changyu Winemaking Company

2. In terms of geographic area, China is considered to be the _____ largest country in the world.
   a. First
   b. Second
   c. Third
   d. Fourth

3. Which of the following areas is located farthest west?
   a. Hebei
   b. Ningxia
   c. Xinjiang
   d. Yunnan

4. Which of the following are the parent grapes of Yan 73?
   a. Muscat Hamburg and Alicante Bouschet
   b. Red Globe and Chenin Blanc
   c. Rose Honey and Chardonnay
   d. Cabernet Sauvignon and Merlot

5. Which of the following grape varieties is a Cabernet Sauvignon X Grenache cross?
   a. Cabernet Gernischt
   b. Marselan
   c. Herbemont
   d. Marufo

6. Which of the following names can be translated as "north of the river"?
   a. Hebei
   b. Shanxi
   c. Yunnan
   d. Dalat

7. Which of the following best describes the location of Ningxia?
   a. On the shores of the Yellow Sea, between Shanghai and Beijing
   b. An island in the Pacific Ocean, to the west of Hong Kong
   c. About 500 miles west of Beijing
   d. In the extreme west of China, on the border with Afghanistan

8. Which of the following is a Chinese wine area located mostly south of the Yangtze River?
   a. Shanxi
   b. Yunnan
   c. Shandong
   d. Kyushu

9. Which of the following best describes the Koshu grape variety?
   a. A pink-skinned grape that is quite successful in Japan
   b. A red hybrid that is used for its intense red color
   c. A red vinifera variety that is grown in Bali
   d. A white labrusca variety that is successful in India's Tamil Nadu region

10. Which of the following is a red hybrid grape, considered to be native to Japan?
    a. Rose Honey
    b. Red Misket
    c. Muscat Bailey-A
    d. Melnik

THE SENSORY EVALUATION OF WINE

CHAPTER TWENTY-ONE

LEARNING OBJECTIVES

After studying this chapter, the candidate should be able to:

- Describe the physiological processes of sight, smell, and taste.
- Identify visual clues concerning a wine's characteristics.

- Recognize the differences between detection threshold and recognition threshold.
- Discuss the differences between aromas, flavors, and taste sensations.
- Recall general procedures for setting up a wine tasting.
- Understand the techniques used in evaluating wine.

EXERCISE 1: UNDERSTANDING THE SENSES: MATCHING

Match each of the following terms with its appropriate definition. Each term will be used only once.

Sweet	Volatile components	Bitter	Umami
Recognition threshold	Perception	Detection threshold	Sensation
Flavor	Olfactory epithelium	Stimulus	

1. _____ A chemical, physical, or thermal activator that can produce a sensory response

2. _____ Molecules that are able to become airborne

3. _____ The neurological response to a stimulus in the environment

4. _____ The brain's interpretation of any information gathered by the senses

5. _____ The smallest amount of a stimulus necessary to trigger an unidentifiable sensation

6. _____ The smallest amount of a stimulus necessary to trigger an identifiable sensation

7. _____ Sensory organ for the sense of smell

8. _____ Term used for the combination of tastes, aromas, and other sensations experienced in wine

9. _____ Humans are most sensitive to this taste component

10. _____ Humans are least sensitive to this taste component

11. _____ The taste of glutamic acid, sometimes referred to as "the protein taste"

Fill in the blanks with an appropriate color descriptor for each style of wine.

WHITE WINE COLORS:

_____ Found in young white table wines from cool growing regions

_____ Found in white wines made from grapes that have not reached optimal ripeness or maturity

_____ The standard hue for most young dry white wines

_____ Found in older white wines

_____ Found in young white wines from warm growing regions

_____ Found in white wines that have spent some time in barrels

_____ May be indicative of a maderized or oxidized white wine

RED WINE COLORS:

_____ Found in young reds

_____ Found in older, mature reds

_____ Found in high-acid reds

_____ Found in low-acid reds

_____ May be indicative of an oxidized red wine

Fill in the blanks for the following statements or questions.

1. The average recognition threshold for sugar in wine is around _____ percent.

2. Very few people will notice the sweetness of a wine with a residual sugar level of _____ or below.

3. The perception of sweetness in a wine can be masked by the presence of _____ or _____.

4. Wine tasters refer to the thickness or viscosity of wine as _____.

5. _____ may be defined as a textural, drying sensation felt on the palate due to the shrinking, puckering, or contraction of the tissues of the mouth.

6. A wine with a high level of alcohol may produce a _____ tactile sensation as well as a _____ taste for some people; hypersensitive tasters may perceive alcohol as a _____ sensation.

7. The term _____ refers to those chemical and physical properties of wine that affect the senses.

8. The umami taste is somewhat rare in wine, but it may be detected in wines that have undergone _____ long enough for the yeast cells to decompose.

9. Wines are often tasted in related groups, known as _____.

10. Some unfiltered or unfined wines may appear cloudy or _____ by design.

11. The size and persistence of the bubbles in a sparkling wine is sometimes referred to as the _____.

12. If there are _____ present in a wine, they will most likely be detected using a "quick sniff" before swirling the glass.

13. The _____ aromas of a wine are often derived from the grape itself, while its _____ aromas may reveal the effects of post-fermentation winemaking techniques such as oak contact or lees aging.

14. Tertiary aromas, often referred to as a wine's _____, are the result of the aging process.

While there is no set standard and many "correct" ways to describe wine, a tasting note should clearly communicate the basic characteristics of a given wine, and—when used to describe wines to customers—should include the information that the customer wants to hear without intimidating or confusing them.

Consider, for example, the following tasting note: "Captain's Winery Monterey County Chardonnay 2020 is a yellow-hued white wine with brilliant clarity. The aromas include green apple, lemon, peach, vanilla, and smoke. It is medium-bodied and dry, with a high level of acidity, medium alcohol, and flavors of peach, green apple, and spice. This is a well-balanced, excellent quality wine with a long finish." Tasting notes such as this can be created using a template—such as the one that follows—as a starting point:

Table 21-1: Suggested Template for a Wine Tasting Note—Example

Characteristic:	Suggested terminology:	Example:
Name of the wine	Include (as applicable) the name of the producer, the type of the wine, the region of origin, and the vintage date	*Captain's Winery Monterey County Chardonnay 2020*
Type	White, Rosé, Red, Fortified, Sparkling	*This is a yellow-hued white wine with brilliant clarity*
Color	White: Yellow/Green, Yellow, Gold Rosé: Pink, Salmon, Orange Red: Purple, Ruby, Garnet, Tawny, Amber, Brown	
Clarity	Dull – Clear - Brilliant	
Aromas	See Appendix D (Wine Aroma Checklist) for possible terminology	*The aromas include green apple, lemon, peach, vanilla, and smoke.*
Sweetness	Dry – Off-dry – Sweet	*This wine is medium-bodied and dry, with a high level of acidity and medium alcohol. The wine has no tannin and no discernible bitterness.*
Acidity	Low – Medium - High	
Bitterness	None – Low – Medium – High	
Tannin	None – Low – Medium – High	
Alcohol	Low – Medium – High	
Body	Light – Medium – Full	
Flavors	See Appendix D (Wine Aroma Checklist) for possible terminology	*The flavors include peach, green apple, and cinnamon.*
Finish	Short – Medium - Long	*The wine has a long finish.*
Other characteristics	Balance, complexity, intensity, or others	*This is a well-balanced, highly complex, and intensely aromatic wine.*
Quality	Poor – Acceptable – Good – Very Good – Excellent	*This is an excellent quality wine.*

Table 21-2: Blank Template for a Wine Tasting Note

Characteristic:	Suggested terminology:	Example:
Name of the wine	Include (as applicable) the name of the producer, the type of the wine, the region of origin, and the vintage date	
Type	White, Rosé, Red, Fortified, Sparkling	
Color	White: Yellow/Green, Yellow, Gold Rosé: Pink, Salmon, Orange Red: Purple, Ruby, Garnet, Tawny, Amber, Brown	
Clarity	Dull – Clear - Brilliant	
Aromas	See Appendix D (Wine Aroma Checklist) for possible terminology	
Sweetness	Dry – Off-dry – Sweet	
Acidity	Low – Medium - High	
Bitterness	None – Low – Medium – High	
Tannin	None – Low – Medium – High	
Alcohol	Low – Medium – High	
Body	Light – Medium – Full	
Flavors	See Appendix D (Wine Aroma Checklist) for possible terminology	
Finish	Short – Medium - Long	
Other characteristics	Balance, complexity, intensity, or others	
Quality	Poor – Acceptable – Good – Very Good – Excellent	

1. On average, a taster will be able to recognize sweetness in a wine if it contains at least _____ residual sugar.
   a. 0.05%
   b. 1%
   c. 2%
   d. 3%

2. Humans are most sensitive to which of the following taste components?
   a. Bitterness
   b. Sweetness
   c. Acidity
   d. Fruitiness

3. Humans are least sensitive to which of the following taste components?
   a. Bitterness
   b. Sweetness
   c. Acidity
   d. Fruitiness

4. Yellow-green hues are most likely to be found in which of the following types of wine?
   a. Older white wines
   b. Young white wines from warm growing regions
   c. White wines that have been barrel-aged
   d. Young white wines from cool growing regions

5. Ruby-orange highlights are most likely to be found in which of the following styles of wine?
   a. Low-acid reds
   b. High-acid whites
   c. High-acid reds
   d. Low-acid whites

6. A turbid appearance is most likely to be found in which of the following styles of wine?
   a. Sparkling wine
   b. Unfiltered wine
   c. Blended wine
   d. High-acid wine

7. Which of the following substances can produce up to three sensory sensations, including a hot tactile sensation, a sweet taste, and a pungent odor?
   a. Tannin
   b. Residual sugar
   c. Alcohol
   d. Tartaric acid

8. Which of the following styles of wine is most likely to be described as astringent?
   a. Mature red Bordeaux
   b. Young Napa Cabernet Sauvignon
   c. Aged white Burgundy
   d. Sauternes

9. Manzanilla Sherry often displays this taste component, which is otherwise somewhat rare in wine:
   a. Saltiness
   b. Sweetness
   c. Acidity
   d. Astringency

10. Which of the following is the source of the umami taste component?
    a. Carbohydrates
    b. Ascorbic acid
    c. Sodium chloride
    d. Amino acids

THE IMPACT OF ALCOHOL ON HEALTH

CHAPTER TWENTY-TWO

LEARNING OBJECTIVES

After studying this chapter, the candidate should be able to:

- Recognize the potential negative consequences of excessive alcohol consumption.
- Discuss the potential health benefits of the moderate intake of alcohol.

- Recall what resveratrol is and how it impacts one's health.
- Understand how to achieve a healthy balance between the risks and benefits associated with alcohol consumption.

EXERCISE 1: THE IMPACT OF ALCOHOL ON HEALTH: FILL IN THE BLANK/SHORT ANSWER

Fill in the blanks for the following statements or questions.

1. _____, the by-product produced when alcohol is metabolized

   in the liver, can build up in the bloodstream and cause_____.

2. _____, defined as consuming large amounts of alcohol one or two nights a week, is one of the leading causes of death among young people.

3. The USDA recommends _____ drink per day for women, and _____ drinks per day for men, as a definition of "moderate consumption."

4. The definition of "one serving" of wine (at 12% to 14% abv) is _____.

5. The definition of "one serving" of beer (at 5% abv) is _____.

6. The definition of "one serving" of spirits (at 40% abv) is _____.

7. Some studies have shown that a decreased risk of coronary heart disease correlates with moderate drinking, most likely due to the _____ and _____-reducing effects of alcohol.

8. It is important to remember that alcohol _____ blood pressure.

9. Excessive amounts of alcohol can lead to _____, a condition where fat accumulates within the cells of the liver.

10. _____ is a nonreversible liver condition that can result from excessive alcohol consumption.

11. _____ is a beneficial phenolic compound found in red wine that has been shown to have anti-aging and disease-fighting properties.

1. Which of the following is considered to be a generally safe level of "moderate drinking," as defined by the USDA?
   a. Up to one drink a day for both men and women
   b. Up to two drinks a day for both men and women
   c. Up to one drink a day for women, and up to two drinks a day for men
   d. Up to one drink a day for men, and up to two drinks per day for women

2. Which of the following is considered to be "one serving" of wine (at 12% to 14% abv), as defined by the USDA?
   a. 4 ounces (118 ml)
   b. 5 ounces (148 ml)
   c. 8 ounces (237 ml)
   d. 10 ounces (296 ml)

3. Which of the following is considered to be "one serving" of beer (at 5% abv), as defined by the USDA?
   a. 12 ounces (355 ml)
   b. 14 ounces (414 ml)
   c. 16 ounces (473 ml)
   d. 20 ounces (591 ml)

4. Which of the following is considered to be "one serving" of spirits (at 40% abv), as defined by the USDA?
   a. ¾ ounce (22 ml)
   b. 1 ounce (30 ml)
   c. 1½ ounces (44 ml)
   d. 2 ounces (59 ml)

5. Which of the following is a beneficial compound often found in red wine and known to have anti-aging and disease-fighting properties?
   a. Flavonols
   b. Acetaldehyde
   c. Methanol
   d. Resveratrol

WINE ETIQUETTE AND SERVICE

CHAPTER TWENTY-THREE

LEARNING OBJECTIVES

After studying this chapter, the candidate should be able to:
- Describe the factors involved in professional wine service, including setup, glassware, opening a bottle, and order of service.
- Understand how temperature, decanting, and storage impact the perceived qualities of a wine.

- Recall the elements of best practices in food and wine pairing.
- Recognize how fat, salt, sweetness, acidity, and bitterness in foods impact the flavors of wine.
- Describe the key actions wine professionals can take to ensure the responsible service of alcohol.

EXERCISE 1: WINE SERVICE: TRUE OR FALSE

Mark each of the following statements as true or false.

1. _____ On a restaurant table, wine glasses should be set to the left of the water glasses.

2. _____ If you need to set glasses while the customer is seated, it is best to place the glasses on the table from the right-hand side of the customer.

3. _____ Soap residue left on flutes will cause the bubbles in a sparkling wine to become agitated and will often cause the glass to overflow.

4. _____ A combination of ice and water will chill wine faster than ice alone.

5. _____ Some people prefer high-acid reds, such as Chianti and Beaujolais, to be served slightly chilled.

6. _____ A bottle of wine that has been ordered by the host should be presented to the host before opening, with the label facing up.

7. _____ After removing the top of the capsule from a bottle of wine, it should be placed on the table or in the ice bucket.

8. _____ Once removed from the bottle, the cork should be placed on the table, to the right of the host.

9. _____ While pouring wine at a restaurant table, it is customary to move clockwise around the table.

10. _____ Upon approval of the wine, the host should always be served first.

11. _____ Using a 5-ounce pour, one standard bottle of wine should easily serve 7 people.

Fill in the blanks or give a short answer for the following statements or questions.

1. When removing the cork from a bottle of sparkling wine, it is advisable to hold the bottle at a _____ degree angle.

2. Let loose, a Champagne cork can fly across the room at _____ mph.

3. Sparkling wines should be served at a temperature of _____.

4. If red wine is served too warm, the taste of _____ may become predominant.

5. The purpose of decanting is to allow a wine's _____ and _____ to develop by exposing it to oxygen.

6. _____ wines may be improved via decanting to soften and mellow out their tannins with exposure to air.

7. Complex wines with _____ aging may be improved by being decanted an hour or two before serving, as this may allow their _____ to open and expand.

8. _____ should be decanted with care and consumed immediately after decanting.

9. Wines with _____ in the bottle should be placed upright for an hour or so before service.

10. _____ white wines such as those produced by Domaine Zind-Humbrecht may improve with decanting to reduce their reductive nature.

11. What is the ideal temperature for a wine cellar?_____

12. What is the ideal level of humidity for a wine cellar? _____

13. Ideal wine storage conditions include storage for the bottles on their side, so that the _____ does not dry out.

Using the term "increases" or "decreases," fill in the blanks in each of the following statements in order to state how a specific food component is expected to impact the perceived flavor of a wine.

The Interaction of Wine and Food	
Food Component:	**Expected impact on wine: Increases or decreases**
Acidity	_____ the perceived acidity of a wine _____ the perceived sweetness of a wine _____ the perceived body (richness) of a wine
Sweetness	_____ the perceived acidity of a wine _____ the perceived sweetness of a wine _____ the perceived fruitiness of a wine _____ the perceived body (richness) of a wine _____ perceived "heat" from spicy food
Saltiness	_____ the perceived fruitiness of a wine _____ the perceived body (richness) of a wine _____ the perceived bitterness of a wine
Bitterness	_____ the perceived bitterness of a wine
Umami	_____ the perceived sweetness of a wine _____ the perceived fruitiness of a wine _____ the perceived body (richness) of a wine _____ the perceived bitterness of a wine

1. Which of the following practices will chill a bottle of wine the fastest?
   a. Placing the bottle in the bottom of the refrigerator
   b. Placing the bottle in the top of the refrigerator
   c. Placing the bottle on ice
   d. Placing the bottle in a combination of ice and cold water

2. Which of the following is the best practice to follow for the table service of wine?
   a. Serve from the customer's left, with the wine glass placed on the left-hand side of the customer's place setting.
   b. Serve from the customer's left, with the wine glass placed on the right-hand side of the customer's place setting.
   c. Serve from the customer's right, with the wine glass placed on the right-hand side of the customer's place setting.
   d. Serve from the customer's right, with the wine glass placed on the left-hand side of the customer's place setting.

3. How many standard 5-ounce pours does a standard 750-ml bottle contain?
   a. Four
   b. Five
   c. Six
   d. Seven

4. Of the following wines, which should be served the coldest?
   a. Dry white Bordeaux
   b. Oregon Pinot Noir
   c. Nonvintage Champagne
   d. Beaujolais Nouveau

5. Of the following wines, which should be served the warmest?
   a. Full-bodied red wines
   b. Light-bodied red wines
   c. Sweet white wines
   d. Full-bodied white wines

6. Which of the following wines may be suitable for decanting?
   a. Young, robust reds
   b. Complex wines with moderate aging
   c. Fully aged, mature red wines
   d. All of the above

7. What are the ideal conditions for a wine cellar?
   a. Cool temperatures between 50°F and 60°F (10°C and 15°C), and humidity of 65–75%
   b. Cool temperatures between 60°F and 70°F (15°C and 21°C), and humidity of 65–75%
   c. Cool temperatures between 50°F and 60°F (10°C and 15°C), and humidity of 30–40%
   d. Cool temperatures between 60°F and 70°F (15°C and 21°C), and humidity of 30–40%

8. During table service, what is the appropriate thing to do once the server has removed the capsule from the top of the wine bottle?
   a. The server should present it to the host.
   b. The server should place it on the table.
   c. The server should place it in an apron or pocket.
   d. The server should place it in an ice bucket.

9. During table service, what is the appropriate thing to do once the server has removed the cork from the bottle?
   a. The server should place it in an apron or pocket.
   b. The server should place it on the table to the right of the host.
   c. The server should hand it to the host.
   d. The server should quickly sniff the cork to see if TCA can be detected.

10. Which of the following practices is advised when opening sparkling wine?
    a. Remove the capsule and the cage before attempting to remove the cork.
    b. Keep the bottle in an ice bucket while removing the cage.
    c. Remove the cork before you chill the bottle.
    d. Hold the bottle at a 45° angle and keep a good grip on the cork.

An answer key for all exercises in this workbook is available on SWE's
"Wine, Wit, and Wisdom" blog site under the "CSW Study Guide Updates" page:
http://winewitandwisdomswe.com/study-guide-updates/csw-updates/csw-workbook-answer-key/

15479409R00109